Science Directions

Year 4

Teaching File

COLLINS

Contents

Introduction	2
4A Moving and Growing	**7**
Activity 1 Bone Location	8
Activity 2 Parts of the Human Skeleton	9
Activity 3 Skeletons of Other Animals	10
Activity 4 Muscles	11
Activity 5 Animals Without Skeletons	12
Key Activity: Do People With the Longest Legs Jump the Furthest or the Highest?	13
Assessment	14
4B Habitats	**15**
Activity 1 Picture Sort	16
Activity 2 School Grounds Survey	17
Activity 3 Invertebrate Survey	18
Activity 4 Food Chains	19
Activity 5 Protection of the Environment	20
Key Activity: Habitat Help	21
Assessment	22
4C Keeping Warm	**23**
Activity 1 Temperature	24
Activity 2 Measuring Temperature Around the School	25
Activity 3 Keeping Things Hot	26
Activity 4 Thermal Insulators	27
Key Activity: Which is the Best Insulator?	28
Assessment	29

4D Solids and Liquids	**31**
Activity 1 Classifying Materials	32
Activity 2 Changing Solids to Liquids	33
Activity 3 Adding Solids to Water: Dissolving	34
Activity 4 Which is the Best Filter?	35
Activity 5 Separating the Mixture	36
Key Activity: Investigating Dissolving	37
Assessment	38
4E Friction	**39**
Activity 1 Forces All Around	40
Activity 2 Measuring Forces	41
Activity 3 Reducing Friction	42
Activity 4 Streamlining	43
Activity 5 Parachutes	44
Key Activity: Which Shoes Give the Best Grip?	45
Assessment	46
4F Circuits and Conductors	**47**
Activity 1 Electrical Circuits	48
Activity 2 Conductors and Insulators	49
Activity 3 Switches	50
Activity 4 Making Use of Electricity	51
Key Activity: What Affects the Brightness of a Bulb?	52
Assessment	53
Photocopiable masters	54

Introduction

Science Directions is a comprehensive and detailed scheme for pupils aged 3–11. It complies completely with the requirements of the Foundation Stage as specified in the Early Learning Goals, and with the Science National Curriculum programmes of study for Key Stages 1 and 2. Science Directions is also matched to the exemplar schemes of work produced by the Qualifications and Curriculum Authority (QCA). Moreover, the time allocations and titles of Science Directions units mirror those in the QCA scheme of work.

Science Directions has a straight-forward structure, comprising one Teaching File and one Pupil Book in each school year from Years 1 to 6. For each unit of work, the Teaching File provides detailed teachers' notes covering a range of activities. Some of the activities are drawn from the QCA schemes of work, others are new and extend the range of experiences for pupils.

Aims

The aims of Science Directions can be summarised as follows:

For Pupils

- to provide a rich and stimulating scientific experience which will foster fascination and interest in science;
- to present science as an essentially practical experience, based largely on first-hand experiences in relevant contexts;
- to develop investigative approaches to scientific enquiry which build confidence in tackling problems with increasing levels of independence;
- to encourage discussion of scientific ideas, and the abilities to question and justify;
- to support a sense of scientific curiosity and the development of appropriate levels of knowledge and understanding.

For Teachers

- to provide an accessible framework of advice and information which closely integrates teacher and pupil material;
- to link the National Curriculum programmes of study to appropriate and interesting activities with a range of possible pupil outcomes;
- to support continuity and progression between different years and key stages, and encourage a constructivist approach in which new ideas are developed from existing ones;
- to encourage the use of questioning to clarify, consolidate and extend understanding;

- to provide explicit links between the activities and National Curriculum levels of attainment, so that assessment of pupil progress can be on-going and informative;
- to support teachers by providing background information on the underlying scientific ideas and principles being developed.

Organisation of the Teaching File

The teaching file includes:

- detailed teacher notes for each unit;
- a set of photocopiable masters for each unit.

Each unit is set out in the following way.

Introductory page of the Unit

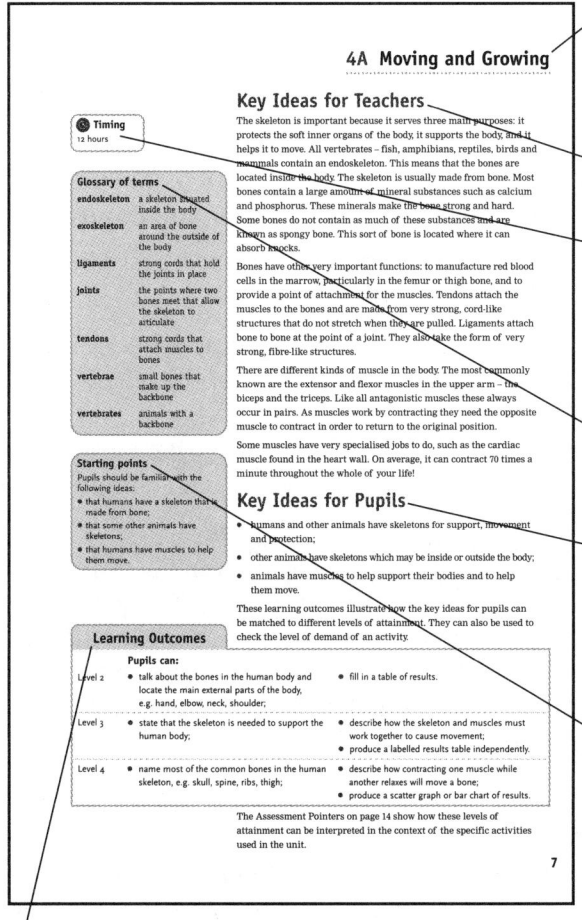

Unit reference and title which matches the QCA scheme of work for science exactly.

Useful background information for Teachers.

The approximate time needed for teaching the unit, based on the recommendations in the QCA scheme of work.

Clear explanations for teachers of key scientific terms relevant to the unit.

Ideas and concepts to be developed which relate directly to the National Curriculum programmes of study for Key Stage 2.

Ideas that pupils will have encountered through their Science Directions work in Key Stage 1.

Typical expectations of pupil attainment for the unit, including those for Sc1 and linked to National Curriculum levels.

Unit Activities

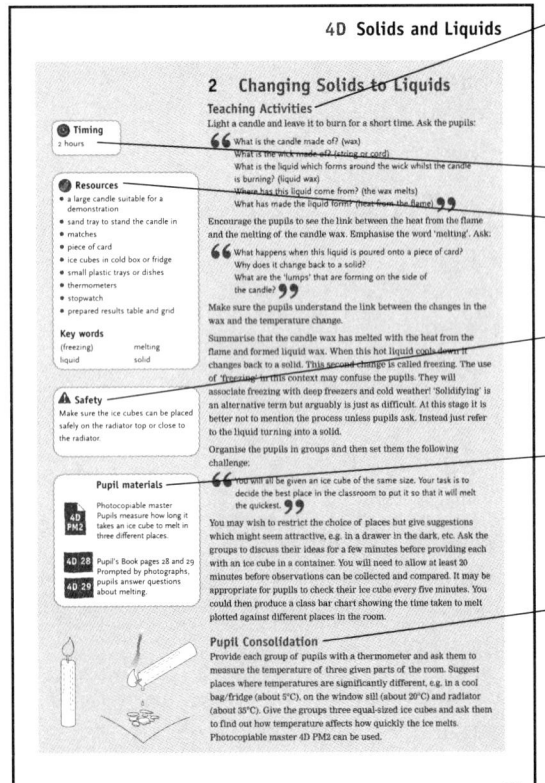

Detailed guidance on how to organise and sequence the various activities. Particular emphasis is given to questions which challenge pupils' thinking and ideas.

The approximate time to cover the activities.

A summary of resources needed and the Key Words that pupils should be introduced to during the activities.

Safety issues specific to the activities. Teachers should always make a risk assessment for the particular group of pupils they are teaching.

Reference to photocopiable masters and pages in the Pupil Book which relate directly to these activities. A summary of each pupil page is given to aid clarity.

Suggestions of other tasks and activities that the pupils can be given to consolidate their learning. In many cases the activities will tend to broaden and extend understanding. As such, they are more likely to be used with selected groups of pupils than with the whole class.

The Key Activity

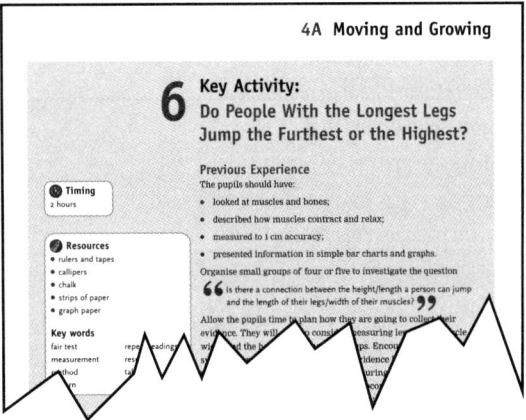

An activity which allows pupils to demonstrate their knowledge, skills and understanding of the unit.

This is usually the final activity in the unit. In almost all cases it provides a specific opportunity to develop and practise Sc1 investigative skills. If required, the activity can also be used to assess pupils' progress in Sc1.

End-of-unit Assessment

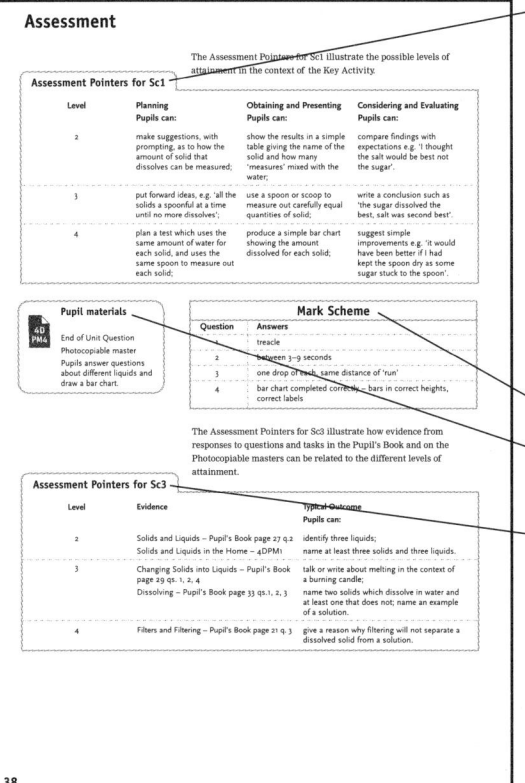

Possible learning outcomes for the Key Activity are provided, as well as some of those given on the first page of the unit. To simplify the assessment process, the learning outcomes are arranged under the 'strands' of planning; obtaining and presenting; considering and evaluating. The outcomes have been written to relate directly to the particular context of the Key Activity and include the type of response expected at each level of attainment. They are not exhaustive and so there will be many other acceptable responses.

Answers to the questions in the end-of-unit test.

Reference to one of the photocopiable masters which can be used as an end-of-unit test.

Indicators of attainment related to the learning outcomes given at the beginning of the unit, placed in the context of questions from the Pupil Book and photocopiable masters. Thus by looking back through the pupil's work, it should be possible to match the work to an overall level of attainment for the unit.

Approaches to Assessment

Science Directions has been designed on the premise that regular assessment of pupil attainment is desirable, and associated feedback to pupils on their progress is important. This does not mean that every piece of work needs to be assessed against National Curriculum levels of attainment. However, if end-of-year judgements are to be made in relation to National Curriculum levels, it is sensible for interim judgements to be carried out similarly.

The approach suggested is to identify certain 'pointers' in each unit which relate to particular 'significant activities', that is, activities which have learning outcomes indicative of a pupil's level of knowledge, understanding or investigative skills. For example, the Key Activity can be seen as a significant activity as it lends itself to the assessment of Sc1. In addition, certain questions in the Pupil Book and on the photocopiable masters can be used as good indicators of levels of attainment.

As judgements on individual pupils are made unit by unit, a profile of attainment emerges and can be established. It is then easy at the end of the year to make an overall judgement on pupil attainment.

A more detailed rationale of the assessment approach, and further advice, can be found in the Co-ordinator's Handbook.

The Pupil Book

Drawings and Photographs

Illustrations are used extensively, not only to convey information, but also to stimulate interest and show the relevance of the scientific ideas being considered.

They should provide a stimulus for discussion and questioning, both with individuals and the class as a whole.

Questions

Questions at the bottom of the page relate directly to the information on the single or double page. Generally the later questions are harder than the earlier ones. They can be used as a basis for whole class discussion or for individual or small group work.

Remember box

This box includes the key facts and ideas that the pupils should be able to recall.

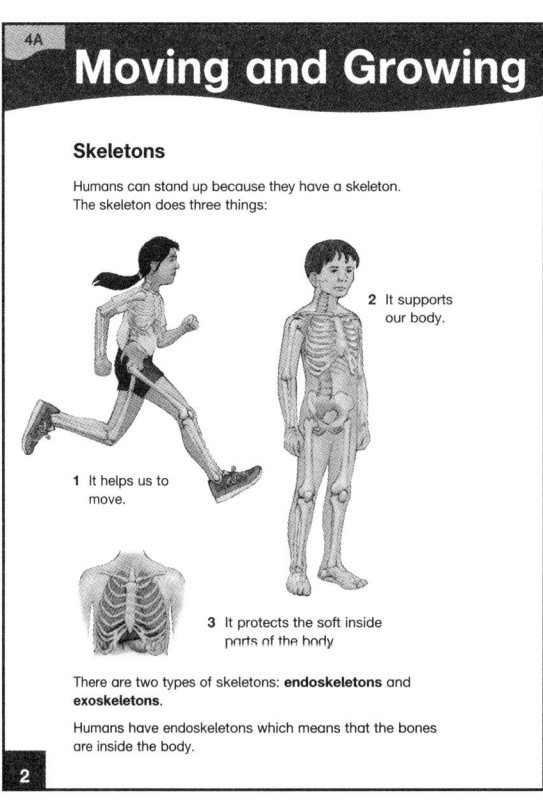

4A Moving and Growing

Timing
12 hours

Glossary of terms

endoskeleton	a skeleton situated inside the body
exoskeleton	an area of bone around the outside of the body
ligaments	strong cords that hold the joints in place
joints	the points where two bones meet that allow the skeleton to articulate
tendons	strong cords that attach muscles to bones
vertebrae	small bones that make up the backbone
vertebrates	animals with a backbone

Starting points

Pupils should be familiar with the following ideas:
- that humans have a skeleton that is made from bone;
- that some other animals have skeletons;
- that humans have muscles to help them move.

Key Ideas for Teachers

The skeleton is important because it serves three main purposes: it protects the soft inner organs of the body, it supports the body, and it helps it to move. All vertebrates – fish, amphibians, reptiles, birds and mammals contain an endoskeleton. This means that the bones are located inside the body. The skeleton is usually made from bone. Most bones contain a large amount of mineral substances such as calcium and phosphorus. These minerals make the bone strong and hard. Some bones do not contain as much of these substances and are known as spongy bone. This sort of bone is located where it can absorb knocks.

Bones have other very important functions: to manufacture red blood cells in the marrow, particularly in the femur or thigh bone, and to provide a point of attachment for the muscles. Tendons attach the muscles to the bones and are made from very strong, cord-like structures that do not stretch when they are pulled. Ligaments attach bone to bone at the point of a joint. They also take the form of very strong, fibre-like structures.

There are different kinds of muscle in the body. The most commonly known are the extensor and flexor muscles in the upper arm – the biceps and the triceps. Like all antagonistic muscles these always occur in pairs. As muscles work by contracting they need the opposite muscle to contract in order to return to the original position.

Some muscles have very specialised jobs to do, such as the cardiac muscle found in the heart wall. On average, it can contract 70 times a minute throughout the whole of your life!

Key Ideas for Pupils

- humans and other animals have skeletons for support, movement and protection;
- other animals have skeletons which may be inside or outside the body;
- animals have muscles to help support their bodies and to help them move.

These learning outcomes illustrate how the key ideas for pupils can be matched to different levels of attainment. They can also be used to check the level of demand of an activity.

Learning Outcomes

Pupils can:

Level 2	• talk about the bones in the human body and locate the main external parts of the body, e.g. hand, elbow, neck, shoulder;	• fill in a table of results.
Level 3	• state that the skeleton is needed to support the human body;	• describe how the skeleton and muscles must work together to cause movement; • produce a labelled results table independently.
Level 4	• name most of the common bones in the human skeleton, e.g. skull, spine, ribs, thigh;	• describe how contracting one muscle while another relaxes will move a bone; • produce a scatter graph or bar chart of results.

The Assessment Pointers on page 14 show how these levels of attainment can be interpreted in the context of the specific activities used in the unit.

4A Moving and Growing

Timing
2 hours

Resources
- large sheets of paper
- large felt pens
- sticky tape or glue
- reference books or CD-ROMs

Key words

bone	shin
hip	skeleton
pelvis	skull
ribs	thigh

Pupil materials

 Pupil's Book pages 2 and 3 show a human skeleton with named bones.

ICT Opportunity
opportunity for research

1 Bone Location

Teaching Activities

This first exercise is designed to find out what the pupils know about bones. Provide the pupils with large pieces of sugar paper or old rolls of wallpaper (use the white side).

Ask pairs to draw around each other, taking turns to lie on the paper, to produce life-sized outlines. Ask the pairs to draw all the bones they think are in the human body within the outline, as near to life size as possible. The pupils' ideas about bones and where they are inside the body will give you a clear indication of any misconceptions they may have (these may include oversized skulls and a very small rib cage). Display these skeleton posters on the classroom wall or hang them from the ceiling for reference. If your class are particularly talented try making 3-D skeletons using paper shapes (the paper can be bent and glued to represent the bones).

Ask the pupils to feel their ribs.

“ How many ribs have you got?
Have we all got the same number?
Is the total the same for everyone? ”

This will cause much discussion as they will find it quite difficult to feel the floating ribs at the bottom of the rib cage.

Challenge them to feel other bones in their bodies and make a list of where they can feel the bones. Compile the results to make a class list. Explain that the pupils will only be able to feel the bones that are near to the surface of the skin. There are many bones in the body that they cannot feel because they are deep inside the body. Pupils should be able to feel knuckles, elbows, ribs, radius, ulna and possibly the top of the pelvic bone over the hips.

Pupil Consolidation

Encourage the pupils to look in reference books and CD-ROMs to find out the names of some of the bones.

Compose a 'bone song' inspired by 'Dem Bones' but make sure it is scientifically accurate! To ensure it is accurate, words such as 'pelvic bone' should be substituted for 'hip bone', 'kneebone' would be 'patella', 'thigh bone' would be 'femur'.

4A Moving and Growing

2 Parts of the Human Skeleton

Teaching Activities

Using a model of a skeleton begin to name the more common bones in the body. Plastic model skeletons are ideal but cardboard ones can be just as scientifically accurate and give the pupils a good idea of scale. The only terms that the pupils need to know at this stage are: skull, rib cage, shoulder blade, backbone, breastbone, pelvis, thigh, calf, arm, foot, hand, toes and fingers. The more enthusiastic pupils might want to use the correct scientific terms but you must ensure they know the common terms too.

Photocopiable master 4APM1 provides a diagram of a skeleton for pupils to label.

If you have some bones available encourage the pupils to handle and talk about them and the way they feel. Ask:

> How does it feel?
> Is it hard or soft?
> Can you bend it?

Clean chicken bones can be used to demonstrate that some bones are very hard (leg bones) and others are flexible (ribs). If a leg bone is cut in half the pupils will be able to see that they are hollow and contain a red material called marrow.

Ask:

> Who has heard the saying 'frozen to the marrow'?

The saying does not actually mean that the marrow is frozen but that the person is feeling cold right the way through their bones!

The pupils may have seen a chicken bone that has been soaked in vinegar in unit 3A Teeth and Eating. This demonstrates how the bone becomes very soft when the calcium has been broken down.

Pupil Consolidation

Research the longest bone ever found. Can the pupils find out which animal it belonged to? Can they find out which animal has the smallest skull?

Timing
2 hours

Resources
- model skeleton
- chicken leg bone

Key words

backbone	foot
breastbone	marrow
calcium	shoulder blade
calf	toes
fingers	

Pupil materials

 Photocopiable master Pupils are given a diagram of a human skeleton to label.

 Pupil's Book pages 2 and 3 shows a skeleton and names common bones.

4A Moving and Growing

3 Skeletons of Other Animals

Teaching Activities

Having looked at a human skeleton, ask:

What do you think the skeletons of other animals might look like? What would a giraffe skeleton look like?

Make a list, e.g. long necks on giraffes, large leg bones on an elephant, tiny finger bones in a squirrel. It would be useful to visit a local museum so the pupils can examine various animal skeletons. If bones from animals are available encourage the pupils to look at them closely and to make close observational drawings. Organise small groups, each with an animal to research using secondary sources.

Questions the pupils could investigate include:

*How many ribs does the animal have?
How many bones are in the neck?
What length are the legs and why might this be?
How is the animal constructed in order to survive in its environment?*

Ask the groups to prepare feedback about their chosen animal to the rest of the class. The feedback should be as active as possible with the pupils demonstrating their information in a variety of ways, including visual aids (e.g. power point presentation, posters, illustrated talk). The best presentations could then form the basis of an assembly.

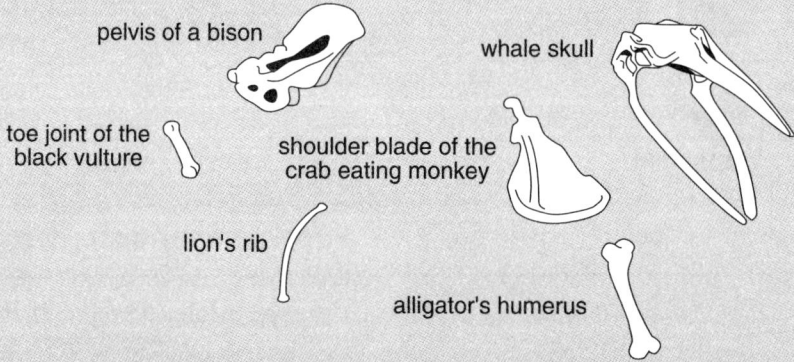

At the end of the session, use a plenary to bring all the ideas together. Establish with the class that skeletons have three main functions. To protect, support and help the body to move.

Timing
2 hours

Resources
- bones
- books or CD-ROM

Key words
adaptation   survive

Pupil materials

4A 4 Pupil's Book pages 4 and 5 illustrates skeletons from a number of different animals.
4A 5

ICT Opportunity
opportunity for Internet research

opportunity for visual display presentation

4A Moving and Growing

4 Muscles

Teaching Activities

Having spent some time looking at bones the pupils will have a clear idea that we have a skeleton for three purposes: protection, support and movement. The exercises described earlier give an indication of how the skeleton offers protection and support and the following activity covers how the skeleton moves.

- Show the pupils an uncooked chicken leg that has had the skin removed. (Turkey would be even better as it is bigger.)
- Flex the leg so that they can see the muscles move.
- Cut away some of the muscle to show how the tendons attach the muscles to the bones.
- Point out that there are many different muscles in the leg and that they always occur in pairs – as one muscle contracts (gets shorter) the other relaxes (gets longer) enabling movement to take place.
- In order for the bones to return to their original position the opposite muscle must contract to pull the bones back into place.

Another way of demonstrating how muscles contract requires a piece of paper approximately 20 cm long; fold it in half and make cuts across the fold that don't quite reach the edge. Open the paper out again and stick the edges together to make a tube. When the tube is in this long, thin state it represents a relaxed muscle. If both ends are pushed together the 'muscle' becomes short and fat and is contracted.

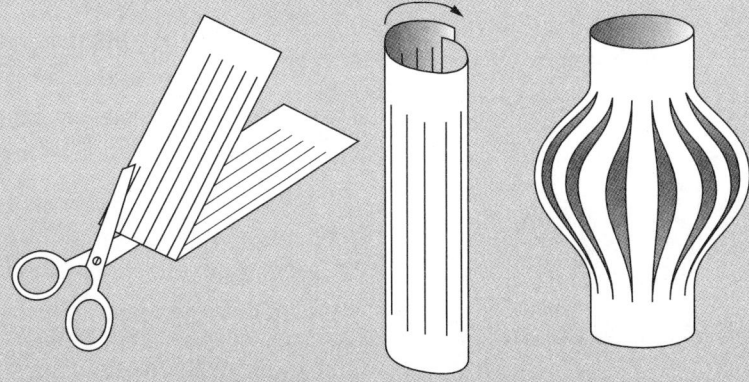

Ask the pupils to hold their upper arm muscles, bend their arm at the elbow and feel one muscle contract (biceps). It is more difficult to feel the underneath muscle (triceps) contracting to stretch the arm out again.

Pupils might like to construct a model of the arm using the Photocopiable master 4APM2 as guidance.

Pupil Consolidation

Research what other types of muscle occur in the human body using CD-ROM or other sources.

Timing
2 hours

Resources
- chicken or turkey leg
- 20 cm long paper
- scissors
- glue
- knife
- CD-ROMs

Key words

contract	pairs
expand	shorten
lengthen	tendon
muscle	

Pupil materials

4A PM2 — Photocopiable master gives pupils a model arm muscle to make.

4A 6 / **4A 7** — Pupil's Book pages 6 and 7 illustrates how muscles work.

Vocabulary
flex (flex your elbow)

ICT Opportunity
opportunity for information retrieval

4A Moving and Growing

Timing
2 hours

 Resources
- pictures of animals with an exoskeleton
- cardboard tubes of three different thicknesses
- paper fasteners
- card
- rubber bands

Key words
external movement
internal muscles

Pupil materials

4A PM2 Photocopiable master
Pupils can construct a model insect leg using the instructions provided.

5 Animals Without Skeletons

Teaching Activities

Ask the pupils to make a quick sketch of what they think an animal without an internal skeleton looks like. Some pupils will produce 'blob' type figures and others might realise that many insects do not have an internal skeleton. Ask:

 What are the advantages of having an internal skeleton?

The main advantages are:
- internal skeletons allow for growth
- animals with external skeletons need to shed them and regularly grow new ones (e.g. insects).

Ask:

 How many of you can name a creature with an external skeleton?

These are known as exoskeleton. These will range from creatures with no visible hard exterior such as worms and slugs, to insects with a hard outer layer (e.g. a beetle). Make clear that all these animals still use muscles in order for them to move – slugs and snails have very strong muscles throughout the length of the body which contract and expand, enabling the animal to move.

Ask:

 How do you think insects can move if they have an exoskeleton? What do you think they need in order to move?

Find out what the pupils think, drawing together their ideas on the board. Tell them in the case of insects, muscles are attached to the inside of the external skeleton, and where a joint occurs the skeleton is slightly softer in order for the joint to be able to move.

Pupils might like to make a model insect leg as described on Photocopiable master 4APM2. Ask them to write an explanation of how movement is possible in animals without an internal skeleton and to give examples of such animals e.g. butterflies, spiders, crabs, lobsters.

4A Moving and Growing

6 Key Activity:
Do People With the Longest Legs Jump the Furthest or the Highest?

Timing
2 hours

Resources
- rulers and tapes
- callipers
- chalk
- strips of paper
- graph paper

Key words
fair test
measurement
method
pattern
repeat readings
results
tables

Pupil materials

Photocopiable master provides a writing frame for pupils to plan and carry out their investigation.

Pupil's Book pages 8 and 9 gives experimental evidence to produce a scatter graph.

Previous Experience
The pupils should have:
- looked at muscles and bones;
- described how muscles contract and relax;
- measured to 1 cm accuracy;
- presented information in simple bar charts and graphs.

Organise small groups of four or five to investigate the question

> Is there a connection between the height/length a person can jump and the length of their legs/width of their muscles?

Allow the pupils time to plan how they are going to collect their evidence. They will need to consider measuring leg length, muscle width and the height and length of jumps. Encourage them to plan a systematic method of recording their evidence by choosing one method of jumping and one way of measuring either leg length or muscle width. You might like to use Photocopiable master 4APM3 which provides a writing frame for this investigation.

After recording data from their own group, prompt the children to gather evidence from other groups who have used similar methods of jumping and measuring. Ask:

> Talk to pupils from other groups, have they obtained results like yours?

Extend the investigation by asking the pupils to compare their conclusions to those of other groups to see if there is a pattern. Ask:

> Is there a pattern in the results?
> Do people with the longest legs jump the furthest?

Finally, encourage each group to produce a scatter graph of the class results.

13

Assessment

The Assessment Pointers for Sc1 illustrate the possible levels of attainment in the context of the Key Activity.

Assessment Pointers for Sc1

Level	Planning Pupils can:	Obtaining and Presenting Pupils can:	Considering and Evaluating Pupils can:
2	decide on how to make their measurements through discussion with the teacher;	use string/paper or other apparatus to make measurements;	compare what they found out with what they expected.
3	independently plan what measurements to take;	use a ruler to take a series of measurements;	identify a simple pattern e.g. long legs jumped higher/further.
4	choose a sensible range of measurements to take;	use a ruler or callipers to measure within 1cm accuracy and communicate these measurements using decimal notation;	suggest how the work could have been improved, e.g. comparing heights jumped with the length of jump.

Pupil materials

End of Unit Question
Photocopiable master
Check pupils' understanding of bones.

Mark Scheme

Question	Answers
1	contract
2	two from, protect, movement, support

The Assessment Pointers for Sc2 illustrate how evidence from responses to questions and tasks in the Pupil's Book and on the Photocopiable masters can be related to the different levels of attainment.

Assessment Pointers for Sc2

Level	Evidence	Typical Outcome Pupils can:
2	Long Legs – Photocopiable master 4APM3	recognise that not everyone has the same-sized bones.
3	Muscles – Pupil's Book page 6 Make a Model Arm – Photocopiable master 4APM2 End of Unit Question: Muscles and Bones – Photocopiable master 4APM4	explain that for movement to occur the muscles must contract.
4	The Human Skeleton – Photocopiable master 4APM1	use scientific names for the bones found in a human skeleton.

4B Habitats

Key Ideas for Teachers

A collection of organisms that live in a particular place is called a community. The actual place that the community occupies is called its habitat, e.g. a forest, seashore, or pond. All the species that occupy the space are part of the habitat, e.g. in a woodland the habitat will contain a community made up from grasses, trees, birds, mammals, etc.

The number of each species collectively are called a population. In the woodland example there will be a population of each type of tree, bird, mammal and ant. The density of this population will depend on the birth rate, death rate and migration of the species. The word 'ecosystem' describes a community and the habitat in which it lives. The living or biotic part of the ecosystem obtains its energy from sunlight and all its raw materials from the non-living, or abiotic, part of the ecosystem.

Sunlight energy is trapped by plants during photosynthesis and is passed via food chains to the entire biotic part of the ecosystem. Most of the energy is eventually lost from the system as heat.

All raw materials that are used, such as nitrogen and carbon, are not lost but are recycled and reused, partly through the action of decomposers. This means that these elements are sometimes part of the biotic element of the system and sometimes part of the abiotic.

Key Ideas for Pupils

- different plants and animals are found in different habitats;
- animals and plants in two different habitats are suited to the particular environment in which they live;
- food chains show the feeding relationships in an ecosystem;
- living things and the environment need protection.

These learning outcomes illustrate how the key ideas for pupils can be matched to different levels of attainment. They can also be used to check the level of demand of an activity.

Timing
12 hours

Glossary of terms

consumers	organisms in a food chain that live by consuming (eating) other organisms
decomposers	fungi and certain bacteria that break down dead organisms
ecosystem	the interaction between the members of a community and its environment
habitat	the part of an environment containing a particular community of organisms
producers	the starting points for a food chain, i.e. green plants

Starting points

Pupils should be familiar with the following ideas:
- that there are different kinds of animals and plants in the local environment;
- that there are differences between local environments;
- that these differences can affect which animals and plants live there.

Learning Outcomes

Pupils can:

Level 2	• identify and name two different habitats, e.g. field, playground, wildlife area;	• make simple observations of snails.
Level 3	• make a record of the different species found in different habitats;	• interpret a diagram showing a simple food chain; • plan a habitat for pond snails.
Level 4	• identify features and characteristics of animals and plants in two different habitats; • explain what is meant by the terms 'predator' and 'prey' and give examples;	• plan to investigate changing factors in a pond environment.

The Assessment Pointers on page 22 show how these levels of attainment can be interpreted in the context of the specific activities used in the unit.

4B Habitats

 **Timing**
2 hours

 **Resources**
- hoops for sorting activity
- reference books and CD-ROMs
- simple keys

Key words

insect	organism
invertebrate	segment
key	wings
legs	

Pupil materials

 Photocopiable master provides pictures of mini-beasts to sort.

 Pupil's Book pages 10 and 11 challenges pupils to follow a key to name some common invertebrates.

Vocabulary
particular

 ICT Opportunity
opportunity for research

1 Picture Sort

Teaching Activities

Ask the pupils what they understand by the term 'organism'. Explain that this word is used to describe living things such as animals and plants.

Provide pictures of plants and invertebrates (animals without a back bone) and say:

 Sort these pictures into sets. You can choose how to put them into sets yourselves.

The pupils can sort them into sets according to their own criteria (numbers of legs, wings, no wings, leaves, shape). You can use Photocopiable master 4BPM1 which provides some suitable pictures. When the pupils have sorted using simple criteria ask them to be more adventurous in their selection (insect, spider, worms, trees, bushes, leaf shape).

 Re-sort the pictures into sets. This time, base your sets on something more scientific, e.g. how the animal moves, or the shape of the plant.

Introduce the idea of some organisms being in more than one group, for example:

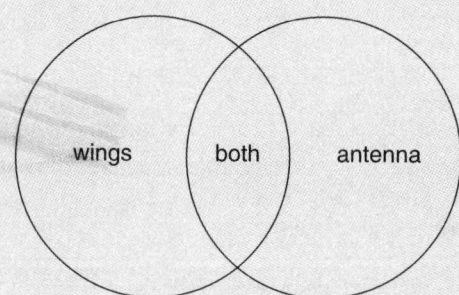

You might like to use hoops to represent the diagram above and ask the pupils to place the pictures of each animal in the correct place in the hoops.

Pose simple questions such as:

 Is it possible for an organism to have wings and not have any legs?

Concentrate on the pictures of invertebrates and ask the pupils to sort them according to their observable features. Some of the pupils may even be able to name them.

Pupil Consolidation

Use reference books and CD-ROMs to identify the pictures of invertebrates.

Use simple keys to identify the organisms using simple yes/no type responses.

4B Habitats

2 School Grounds Survey

Teaching Activities

Ask the pupils what they understand by the term 'habitat'. Write their ideas on the board (e.g. it's where an animal lives, it has plants in it, it can be destroyed.). Explain that there are many different kinds of habitat, some of which they might only have seen on television, e.g. rainforest, desert. Point out that there are many different kinds of habitat around the school such as flower borders, the school field and playground. Ask the pupils to make a list of all the habitats they can think of.

Take the pupils around the grounds or a nearby park, and using Photocopiable master 4BPM2, ask them to list all the habitats they can find. Back in the classroom discuss the size of the habitats that have been identified and order them according to size, e.g. a pond and a flower border may be roughly the same size.

Ask:

> What kinds of organisms do you think might live in each habitat? Will we find the same organisms in the pond as we will on the school field?

Explain to the pupils that they are going to undertake a habitat survey and in order to do that they need to be able to catch the invertebrates that live there.

Prompt the pupils to think of ways in which they could catch the organisms. Fingers are not an option! Show the pupils simple catching devices such as soft paintbrushes and sample bottles, or pond dipping nets and white trays. Ask the class to compile a list of rules for the safe collection of invertebrates. Examples are, do not touch with hands; use a soft brush for collection; use a container that invertebrates can breath in; always return to where they were found.

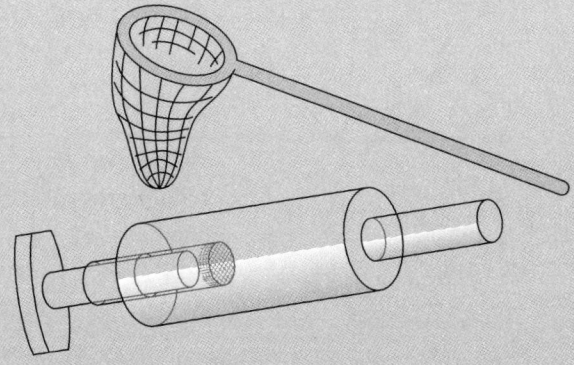

Pupil Consolidation

Help the pupils to sort leaves (from bushes and small plants) according to observable features (e.g. number of lobes on the leaf, shape of the veins, whether they have serrated leaves or not) and then attempt to name the plant they came from using a simple key.

Timing
2 hours

Resources
- pond dipping equipment
- hand lenses
- pooters
- bug boxes
- soft paintbrushes
- sample bottles
- white trays
- simple key for leaves

Key words

habitat   organism
invertebrate   survey

Pupil materials

 Photocopiable master provides a format for pupils to record their habitat survey on.

 Pupil's Book pages 12 and 13 describes a pond dipping expedition.

Vocabulary
suited to

17

4B Habitats

Timing
2 hours

Resources
- invertebrate survey equipment as listed for the previous activity
- simple keys
- graph paper
- simple key for trees

Key words
common   invertebrates
habitat

Pupil materials

  Pupil's Book pages 14 and 15 illustrates a data handling exercise.

Vocabulary
variety

ICT Opportunity
opportunity for visual display presentation

3 Invertebrate Survey

Teaching Activities

Recap the list of safe methods for catching invertebrates from the last session. Ask small groups to select a habitat to survey and then make predictions as to what they may find there (don't forget the plants!). Ask:

 What do you think you will find in the flower border?
What will be in the log pile?

The groups should then observe the area for half an hour to see what can be found. Encourage them to make notes outside, and to make a permanent record (in their exercise books or on a poster) of what they found when they return to the classroom.

They will need to produce a plan of their chosen habitat and on it show where they found various organisms. Display the plans on the classroom wall and, as a class, discuss the surveys of the different groups, comparing and contrasting the habitats and the organisms found. Ask:

 Did you find the same creatures in the log pile as in the flower border?
Why do you think this was?
Did you find the same plant species in different habitats?

Produce a chart showing the class totals for the survey, indicating numbers for the whole school habitat, for example:

Habitat	Oak trees	Woodlice	Greenfly
Playground	10	2	0
Pond	0	5	12
Flower border	2	20	50
Totals	12	27	62

Ask the groups to choose ways to present the group and class data, e.g. pie charts, bar charts, tally charts. This provides a good opportunity to use ICT to record and display the data.

Pupil Consolidation

Identify the most common trees found around the school site by using a simple key.

4B Habitas

Timing
2 hours

Resources
- food chains
- paper and string to make a mobile
- video of nature programme on food chains

Key words

consumer	predator
food chain	prey
organism	producer

4 Food Chains

Teaching Activities

Ask the pupils to list what they had to eat yesterday. Ask:

❝ How was the food you ate yesterday manufactured?
Do you know where it came from? ❞

Explain that the pupils are going to construct food chains for various different habitats. Start by showing a simple food chain on the board:

grass → rabbit → fox

If the words 'is eaten by' is placed above the arrows this might help the pupils understand and remember the notation.

Ask the pupils to research what eats what by using secondary sources. It is easier to start with chains that contain large animals e.g.:

grass → gazelle → lion

Introduce the terms 'predator' and 'prey'. Explain that a predator is something that eats prey. Use the rabbit → fox example, the rabbit is the prey and the fox is the predator. Ask the pupils to identify predators and prey in given food chains. Remind them of the kinds of organisms that they found in their habitat survey. They should research further to find out what invertebrates eat and what eats them. Then ask the pupils to construct food chains for the organisms that they found around the school in a given habitat, e.g. the flower bed. Having chosen a food chain to illustrate, pupils could construct a mobile created from their own drawings of the various organisms. The mobiles should show the consumers at the top and the producers underneath. Remember that all food chains begin with a green plant. The mobiles can be suspended from the classroom ceiling.

Pupil Consolidation

Using video material as a stimulus, ask the pupils to write a script for a wildlife programme which focuses on a simple food chain.
Encourage the pupils to make their script as detailed as possible.

4B Habitats

5 Protection of the Environment

Teaching Activities

This session is best taught around a pertinent, topical environmental issue. If there is nothing in the news then a scenario will need to be invented.

For example, you could ask the pupils:

> "Would draining the school pond and replacing it with an adventure playground be a good idea?
> What would happen to the organisms that live in and around the pond?"

Some pupils will think this a good idea. Others would be more concerned that the animals living in the pond would die.

Alternatively, ask the class to consider what would happen to a nearby woodland if all the trees were felled. Again the effects on the organisms should be considered including the plants.

Divide the class into two groups: ask one group to prepare an illustrated debate in favour of a particular proposal, and the other half the argument against. Encourage the teams to find out as much information as possible on the chosen issue, and to prepare poster material to illustrate their case. Ideally this should be something topical, e.g. a road widening scheme, or building on green site land. This can be changed year on year to reflect local issues. If there are no local issues to debate, then the school pond scenario could be used.

Establish what the rules for debate are (no shouting out; listen to others points of view; the teacher acts as chair person) and allocate each side a finite amount of time (e.g. 5 minutes) in which to present their case. It might be a good idea to have a small panel of Year 6 pupils present to decide which side has presented the most convincing case, and explain why.

Pupil Consolidation

Prompt the pupils to write a newspaper article to support a local environmental issue for display in the entrance to the school.

Timing
2 hours

Resources
- newspaper cuttings of current environmental issues

Key words
argument   pollution
environment

Pupil materials

Pupil's Book pages 16 and 17 raises the issue of habitat destruction.

4B Habitats

6 Key Activity: Habitat Help

Timing
2 hours

Resources
- large jars
- pond dipping equipment
- access to pond life (snails)
- pond weed
- gravel

Key words

bottom	light
conditions	observe
dark	plants (elodea, hornwort)
diary	
food	snails

⚠ Safety
Pupils must be closely supervised during pond dipping type activities. They should be warned about washing their hands thoroughly after being in contact with pond water.

Pupil materials

Photocopiable masters provide a blank pond diary for pupils to complete.

Previous Experience
The pupils should have:
- made simple observations;
- planned a simple experiment;
- recorded results in a table;
- looked for patterns in their results.

Discuss with the class what they would expect to find in the school/local pond. List the possible plants and animals, and then ask the pupils:

 Why do these animals live in water?

Possible answers include, because they are suited to the environment, e.g. webbed feet, gills etc.

Then list the features of pond-living animals e.g. some have gills, they can swim, they have webbed feet.

Explain to the pupils that they are going to collect some pond animals, e.g. snails, and investigate the conditions in which they live.

Explain that a pond is a miniature world in which the lives of the plants and animals are linked by food chains. Tell the pupils that they are going to be making a miniature pond to enable them to observe some plants and animals in the classroom. You will need a large jar for each group (sweet jars are ideal).

Each group should place gravel or some other suitable material in the bottom of the jar and then fill it with pond water, adding some pond weed (elodea or hornwort). Two or three small herbivores should then be placed in the jar – small pond snails or ramshorn snails are good ones to try. The lid should be loosely fitting and the bottle ponds checked daily for 5 days to observe the condition of the water and the organisms in it.

Encourage the pupils to pose questions (on paper) about what conditions the pond snails prefer –

 Do they live near the edge or near the middle of the pond?
Do they live under leaves?
What do they eat?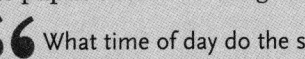

The pupils should investigate their ideas over a period of a week. Ask:

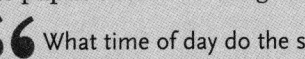 What time of day do the snails move?
Are they near the tops or bottom first thing in the morning?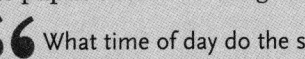

Photocopiable master 4BPM3 provides a useful frame for a 'pond diary'. (The Photocopiable master consists of two pages which should be photocopied back to back in order to make the pond diary.)

Assessment

The Assessment Pointers for Sc1 illustrate the possible levels of attainment in the context of the Key Activity.

Assessment Pointers for Sc1

Level	Planning Pupils can:	Obtaining and Presenting Pupils can:	Considering and Evaluating Pupils can:
2	plan to collect the snails carefully;	make simple observations about the way in which the snails move;	make a simple comparison of two types of snail.
3	plan to provide the snails with the correct habitat, e.g. plants, gravel, water;	observe the snails appear to be towards the top of the jar in the morning and the bottom in the afternoon;	state that the ramshorn snails moved more than the other types.
4	independently plan to investigate the effect of changing one factor in the habitat, e.g. light/dark conditions;	make a series of time measurements which plot the path of the snails in the jar;	identify the patterns in the way the snails move.

Pupil materials

End of Unit Question
Photocopiable master
Tests pupils understanding of food chains and pond animal adaptations.

Mark Scheme

Question	Answers
1	sensible rules
2	reproduce, move, grow
3	plants → tadpoles → caddis fly or diving beetle

The Assessment Pointers for Sc2 illustrate how evidence from responses to questions and tasks in the Pupil's Book and on the Photocopiable masters can be related to the different levels of attainment.

Assessment Pointers for Sc2

Level	Evidence	Typical Outcome Pupils can:
2	Pond Dipping – Pupil's Book page 13	state that different living things are found in different places, e.g. pond.
3	Habitat Survey – Photocopiable master 4BPM2	name organisms that can be found in two different habitats.
4	Pond Dipping – Pupil's Book page 13	construct simple food chains.

4C Keeping Warm

Timing
10 hours

Glossary of terms

conduction	the transfer of thermal energy through a solid
temperature	the number of degrees of hotness of an object
thermal conductor	a substance that allows thermal energy to pass through it
thermal insulator	a substance that does not allow thermal energy to pass through it

Starting points

Pupils should be familiar with the following ideas:

- a thermometer is used to measure temperature;
- that materials can be sorted into groups on the basis of their properties;
- that materials are chosen for particular uses as a result of their properties.

Key Ideas for Teachers

A thermometer is made with a liquid with a high coefficient of expansion, i.e. a liquid which expands quite significantly even for a small change in temperature. The safest liquid to use in a thermometer is alcohol.

Thermal energy is transferred through a solid by the process of conduction. A solid is made up of particles (usually atoms or molecules) which are constantly vibrating and bumping into each other. If one end of the material is warmed, the particles at that end will start to vibrate more vigorously and will bump into neighbouring particles, making them vibrate more vigorously too. In this way the thermal energy is transferred through the material by vibrating particles. The structure and arrangement of particles in some materials means that the energy travels very quickly – these are the good conductors.

If a thermometer is held in a warm liquid, particles in the liquid will bump into the glass bulb of the thermometer. The glass particles will vibrate more and transfer the thermal energy through to the alcohol. The particles in the alcohol will move around more quickly and take up more space – the liquid expands and a higher temperature is recorded.

Key Ideas for Pupils

- temperature is a measure of how hot or cold things are;
- some materials are better thermal insulators than others;
- some materials are better electrical conductors than others.

These learning outcomes illustrate how the key ideas for pupils can be matched to different levels of attainment. They can also be used to check the level of demand of an activity.

Learning Outcomes

Pupils can:

Level 2	• recognise that temperature measures how hot or cold objects are; • use thermometers to measure temperature;	• identify some everyday uses of thermal insulators; • make simple comparisons.
Level 3	• identify some materials which are good thermal insulators and some everyday uses of these;	• recognise that some materials keep cold objects cold and warm objects warm; • plan an approach to an investigation.
Level 4	• recognise that objects cool or warm to the temperature of their surroundings when they are left;	• recognise that metals are both good thermal and electrical conductors; • support conclusions with scientific explanations.

The Assessment Pointers on page 29 show how these levels of attainment can be interpreted in the context of the specific activities used in the unit.

4C Keeping Warm

Timing
2 hours

Resources
- three bowls, access to hot and cold water
- alcohol thermometers or alternative
- a range of other types of thermometer, including the liquid crystal 'forehead' type and a temperature sensor attached to a data logger and computer
- containers (preferably insulated, e.g. polystyrene cups and lids) for different samples of water
- labelled polystyrene cups containing: A iced water, B cold water, C hot tap water, D tea, E soup, F instant noodle meal

Key words

Celsius	sensor
colder	temperature
(Fahrenheit)	thermometer
hotter	

Safety
If a kettle is used to provide hot water add sufficient cold water to ensure that the pupils don't scald themselves.

Warn the pupils to handle the thermometers very carefully – they are very fragile.

Pupil materials

Photocopiable master
Pupils use a thermometer to test the temperature of various liquids.

Pupil's Book pages 18 and 19
Pupils decide which thermometer is suited to a particular use and estimate temperatures.

1 Temperature

Teaching Activities

The pupils may have encountered the characteristic properties of materials and the melting of ice in Unit 3C. In this unit the intention is to develop the concept of thermal conductors and insulators, and to extend the use of thermometers for making accurate measurements of temperature.

The first part of this activity demonstrates that while the human body notices *differences* in temperature, it is not very good at judging temperature itself.

Set up three bowls in a line. Put hot water (not too hot) in an outside bowl and cold water in the other outside bowl. Put warm water in the middle bowl. Ask a pupil to put one of their hands in each of the outside bowls for 30 seconds. Ask the pupil to describe what their hands feel like. After 30 seconds ask the pupil to put both hands in the centre bowl. Ask them what their hands feel like now.

The hand that has been in hot water should feel quite cold, the other hand should feel quite warm. Ask the class:

 Can the same water have different temperatures?

Ask the pupil to take the temperature of the water in the middle bowl. Ask:

 Can you predict roughly the temperature of the water?
Why does the water in the middle bowl feel so different?

Give other examples of how the body copes with dramatic changes in temperature, e.g. when you come inside after being outside in the cold you often feel really warm for the first few minutes, etc.

Check the pupils know that temperature is measured in degrees Celsius. Provide each pupil or group with a thermometer. Provide a range of 'water samples' (see Resources) for them to measure. Encourage them to predict the temperature before they measure it. Photocopiable master 4CPM1 can be used to support this activity. Talk about the dangers of scalding with foods like soup and instant noodle meals.

Show the pupils other types of thermometers, e.g. soil thermometer, clinical thermometer, liquid crystal 'forehead' thermometer, temperature sensor linked to a computer. Discuss how they are used and the advantages of each. Mention that some thermometers still measure in degrees Fahrenheit. Set up a temperature probe to a data logger and computer, and leave it to monitor room temperature over a period of 24 hours. (You will need these results for Activity 2.)

Pupil Consolidation

Prompt the pupils to research different types of thermometer. For each type they could draw a diagram, write a sentence to explain how it is used and say why it is useful.

4C Keeping Warm

2 Measuring Temperature Around the School

Teaching Activities

Look at the trace of the temperature against the time graph produced by the temperature sensor and the computer. Add the times of the day to the time axis to help interpretation. Ask the pupils why they think the temperature changed. Ask:

 At what time was the temperature the highest?
Can you think of a reason?
At what time was the temperature the lowest?
Can you think of a reason?

Can the pupils tell from the graph at what time the heating switched on/the sun started to shine/it got dark?

Ask the pupils to predict the current room temperature. Provide each pupil or groups with a thermometer and ask them to measure room temperature. Do they know why they shouldn't hold the thermometer around the bulb when taking temperatures?

Show the pupils a weather chart from a newspaper. Discuss how it shows the temperature in different parts of the country. Talk about the types of temperatures in Britain during the day in summer and in winter.

Provide the pupils with a simple plan of the school showing the main parts of the building. Ask each group to choose ten different parts of the school where they think the temperatures might be different. Encourage them to think of places that are usually hot, cold, seem about right, etc. They should choose places where they will be able to take temperatures without disturbing other classes. To cover a good range of temperatures they might need to go outside the school buildings. Ask the pupils to take temperatures at ten places and record the results in a simple table. Remind them that it might take a minute before the thermometer has adjusted to a change in temperature.

Once they have taken the temperatures the pupils can complete a 'weather map' of the school showing the temperatures at various points on the plan. Ask the pupils to tell you where the 'hot spots' and the 'cold spots' are, and to suggest reasons for these differences.

Pupil Consolidation

Prompt the pupils to look at the weather section of a newspaper. Can they find the temperature of a city in France, Spain, Italy, USA, Africa and Australia? Ask them to write down the cities in order of temperature, starting with the coldest and finishing with the hottest.

 **Timing**
2 hours

 Resources
- computer print-out showing room temperature over a 24-hour period
- thermometers
- weather maps from newspapers
- a simple plan of the school
- access to newspapers with temperatures of cities across the world

Key words

Celsius   temperature
constant   varied
sensor

 Safety
Warn the pupils not to let the thermometers roll off the tables.

 Pupil materials

 Pupil's Book pages 20 and 21
Pupils interpret weather maps to predict temperatures.

Vocabulary
eventually

 ICT Opportunity
opportunity for data gathering

4C Keeping Warm

3 Keeping Things Hot

Teaching Activities

Decide on what you are going to ask the pupils to keep hot. A jacket potato works well but there are many other alternatives.

Explain that the staff are going to have a party at the end of the day but need to keep the jacket potatoes warm until then. Show the pupils how a small hole can be made in the potato (using scissors) and a thermometer inserted to take the temperature. Show them a range of materials to surround the potato. Ask the pupils which material will be the best for keeping the potato hot.

Make a list of their suggestions on the board. Then allocate a different material to each group. Try and restrict the number of materials tested to six. You might like to introduce a few rules, e.g. you can only cover the potato with two layers of the material. Discuss the approach to be used. It is important that all groups use the same basic method in order that the results can be compared. Photocopiable master 4CPM2 can be used to guide the investigation.

 Timing
2 hours

 Resources
- hot jacket potatoes (access to an oven, insulated box)
- a range of potential insulating materials including: newspaper, fabric, plastic, kitchen roll, etc. – see activity notes
- scissors
- thermometers
- clock or stopwatches

Key words
conductor   thermal
insulator   thermometer
temperature

 Safety
Warn the pupils of the dangers of burning themselves on the hot potato.

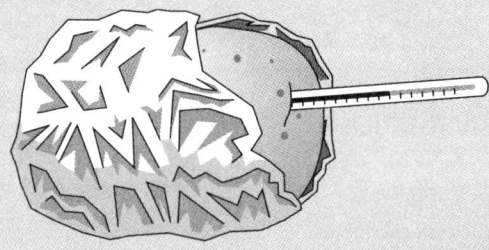

Pupil materials

 Photocopiable master Pupils find the best insulator by using different materials to keep something hot.

 Pupil's Book pages 22 and 23
 Pupils identify thermal insulators and thermal conductors and contrast thermal and electrical conductors.

When each group has collected its results collect them on a master chart and draw a bar chart to represent the results. Introduce the words 'conductor' and 'insulator' and explain what they mean. Some pupils might remember that 'conductor' is used in the context of electricity. Encourage the pupils to use the word 'thermal' to distinguish the two types of conductor. Discuss the findings, asking:

 Which material kept the potato the hottest?
Which material let the potato cool down the quickest?

Can the pupils conclude which material is the best conductor and which the best insulator?

Note: Care will be needed with aluminium foil. It is a metal and so is a good conductor of heat. However, it is effective at keeping potatoes warm because, as a reflective surface, it reduces energy transfer by radiation. If you think this will cause confusion then don't include this as a material to test.

ICT Opportunity
opportunity for research

Pupil Consolidation

Ask the pupils if they know what a thermos flask is and what it is used for. Can they find out what materials it is made from?

4C Keeping Warm

4 Thermal Insulators

Teaching Activities

Remind the pupils of the sorts of materials that keep things hot. Ask them the terms used to describe materials that keep things hot and materials that don't keep things hot.

Ask the pupils what type of clothes make good insulators (to keep you warm). Examples include woollen scarves, jumpers, gloves, etc. Provide a few magazines and ask the pupils to cut out examples of clothes that act as good insulators.

Show the pupils an ice box and ask them what it is used for (to keep things cold). Show the pupils any other insulated bags, boxes or drinks canisters that are used for keeping things cold. Encourage them to look carefully at the sorts of material. Ask the pupils to make a list of materials that are used to keep things cold. Explain that these are also called insulators. So an insulator is something that keeps something warm or cold.

Stand a wooden, a metal and a plastic spoon in a pan of very hot water. After several minutes ask the pupils which spoon will feel the hottest and which the coolest. Can they tell you which material is the best insulator? Ask one of the pupils to feel the spoons to see if the predictions were correct. Show the pupils a saucepan with a wooden or plastic handle and ask:

What is the handle made of?
Why has this material been used?

Ask the pupils to look through magazines and cut out examples of things made from thermal insulating materials and conducting materials. The pupils can glue their cuttings into a table:

thermal insulators	thermal conductors

Pupil Consolidation

Prompt the pupils to find out about electrical conductors, and what types of materials are used to conduct electricity.

Timing
2 hours

Resources
- examples of ice boxes, insulated bags and canisters, drinks containers
- magazines
- scissors, glue
- a pan of very hot water
- a pan with a wooden or plastic handle
- a kettle (for boiling water)
- spoons – wooden, plastic and metal

Key words
conductor   thermal
insulator

Pupil materials

Pupil's Book pages 24 and 25
Pupils identify appropriate thermal insulators for particular uses.

Vocabulary
reduces

ICT Opportunity
opportunity for research

4C Keeping Warm

5 Key Activity: Which is the Best Insulator?

Timing
2 hours

Resources
- ice cubes of uniform size
- scissors
- four different types of insulating materials, including wool, cotton, newspaper, toilet paper. Avoid plastic, bubble wrap, etc. unless the weighing method is to be used.
- rubber bands
- paper towels
- (weighing scales)

Key words
insulator   melting

Pupil materials

Photocopiable master
Pupils use a writing frame to guide their investigation on insulating materials.

Previous Experience

The pupils should have:
- made supported predictions;
- used fair tests;
- supported conclusions with scientific reasons.

Provide the pupils with four different materials to compare. The idea is to wrap four identical ice cubes in the same amount of four different materials and see how quickly the ice cubes melt.

One of the problems is how to measure the extent of the melting. If the materials chosen are porous, one way is to put the wrapped cube in the centre of a paper towel and compare the size of the water stains as the cube melts. Another possibility is to weigh the cubes but this does present problems of unwrapping the ice cubes (also the balance used may not be accurate enough to give clear differences).

Pupils might suggest measuring the cubes with a ruler or simply waiting until the ice has completely melted. The difficulty with this last approach is that it is difficult to judge when the ice has completely gone.

Make sure you allow time for initial discussion of the problem and encourage the pupils to explain their ideas. During this discussion leave an ice cube on the table so the pupils begin to appreciate that it melts quite slowly even when not covered. Suggest the 'paper towel' method if you think it is appropriate.

The writing frame provided on Photocopiable master 4CPM3 can be used to support the pupils in their investigation. Give the pupils time to complete the planning part before they start the investigation.

The pupils should be able to present their results in a number of ways, including cutting around the water stains that form on the paper towels.

When individual groups have put the materials in order of effectiveness it is worth discussing why all groups didn't get the same order. The pupils may be able to suggest improvements to the approach to make it more reliable.

Assessment

The Assessment Pointers for Sc1 illustrate the possible levels of attainment in the context of the Key Activity.

Assessment Pointers for Sc1

Level	Planning Pupils can:	Obtaining and Presenting Pupils can:	Considering and Evaluating Pupils can:
2	with prompting suggest how to compare the four different materials;	make simple comparisons, e.g. 'the ice cube covered in the cotton melted quicker than the one covered in the wool';	compare findings with expectations, e.g. 'I was wrong. I thought the wool would be the best'.
3	design an approach that will enable the best insulator to be found, including how to measure the amount of melting that occurs;	measure the size of the water 'stain' on the paper towel;	identify the order in which the ice cubes melted.
4	make a supported prediction as to which material will make the best insulator, e.g. 'I think the wool will be the best because it is an insulator in clothes';	perform a fair test making sure that the ice cubes are all the same size, and the same amount of insulating material is used;	support conclusions with scientific reasons, e.g. 'the wool was the best insulator as it trapped the most air'.

Pupil materials

End of Unit Question
Photocopiable master
Pupils match conditions and temperatures and consider the importance of room temperature.

Mark Scheme

Question	Answers
1	cool water 15°C, water and ice 0°C, hot water 60°C, warm water 40°C
2	it will melt
3	18°C, 18°C

The Assessment Pointers for Sc3 illustrate how evidence from responses to questions and tasks in the Pupil's Book and on the Photocopiable masters can be related to the different levels of attainment.

Assessment Pointers for Sc3

Level	Evidence	Typical Outcome Pupils can:
2	Taking Temperatures – Photocopiable master 4CPM1	use a thermometer to measure different temperatures;
	Thermal Insulators – Pupil's Book page 23 q.3	identify a use for plastic foam.
3	More Thermal Insulators – Pupil's Book page 25 qs.1, 2, 3	name suitable materials for use in an oven glove, to surround a water tank and to make a 'cool box'.
4	Temperature – 4CPM4 q.3	appreciate that the temperature of both jars of water would become 18°C.

29

4D Solids and Liquids

Timing
11 hours

Key Ideas for Teachers

In a solid the particles are held together in a regular pattern which gives the solid its shape. In a liquid the particles are more randomly arranged and are generally slightly further apart than they are in a solid (ice and water are an exception to this simple model). The lack of regularity in a liquid, and the fact that the forces between the particles tend to be less than those in a solid, means that a liquid will flow and take the shape of any container it is poured into.

When a solid is heated, the particles gain energy and vibrate more rapidly until, at the melting point, the vibrations are sufficient to break the forces that exist between the particles and the solid melts. When a liquid is cooled the particles move more slowly and move closer together until, at the freezing point, they are moving slowly enough to link together in a regular pattern.

When a solid is added to water, the water particles surround the solid particles at the edge of the solid structure. If the attractions between the water particles and the solid particles are greater than the attraction between the solid particles themselves, then the solid will dissolve, forming a solution. As a solid can only dissolve if water particles completely surround each solid particle there will always be a limit to how much solid can be dissolved in a fixed amount of water. When no more solid will dissolve the solution is said to be saturated.

Glossary of terms

dissolving	the process in which a solid mixes closely with a liquid so individual solid particles cannot be seen
filtering	the process of using a porous material to separate a solid from a liquid
freezing	the process whereby a liquid changes into a solid
melting	the process whereby a solid turns into a liquid
saturated	a solution which will not dissolve any more solid at a particular temperature
solution	the substance formed when a solid dissolves in a liquid

Key Ideas for Pupils

- to recognise the differences between solids and liquids in terms of ease of flow and maintenance of shape and volume;
- mixing materials, e.g. adding salt to water, can cause them to change;
- some solids, e.g. salt and sugar, dissolve in water to give solutions but some, e.g. sand and chalk, do not;
- insoluble solids can be separated from liquids by filtering.

These learning outcomes illustrate how the key ideas for pupils can be matched to different levels of attainment. They can also be used to check the level of demand of an activity.

Starting points

Pupils should be familiar with the following ideas:
- materials can be sorted into groups on the basis of simple properties, e.g. appearance and texture;
- everyday materials such as water, chocolate, bread and clay change when they are heated or cooled.

Learning Outcomes

Pupils can:

Level 2	• name some solids and liquids; • describe that when ice melts it turns into a liquid;	• state that salt and sugar dissolve in water but sand does not; • show results in a simple table.
Level 3	• describe the differences between solids and liquids; • use the terms 'melting' and 'dissolving';	• explain that undissolved solids can be separated from liquids by filtering; • measure quantities accurately.
Level 4	• state that some solids, e.g. metals, have high melting points; • plan a fair test;	• explain that a solution passes through a filter paper because the solid particles have been broken down by the water to a very small size.

The Assessment Pointers on page 38 show how these levels of attainment can be interpreted in the context of the specific activities used in the unit.

4D Solids and Liquids

Timing
1½ hours

Resources
A wide range of materials including
- wood, metal, glass, plastic, paper, card
- sand, salt, sugar (granular and lump), flour, talcum powder
- water, lemonade, cola, washing-up liquid, tea, coffee
- tomato sauce as a viscous liquid
- glasses or vases of different shapes

Key words

coloured	powder
colourless	property
crystals	solid
liquid	

Safety
This is a good opportunity to emphasise the importance of not playing with liquids other than water at home. Many of the liquids used at home are hazardous.

Pupil materials

4D PM1 Photocopiable master
Pupils find different types of solids and liquids.

4D 26 / **4D 27** Pupil's Book pages 26 and 27
Pupils identify materials with particular properties and, prompted by photographs, look at the properties of liquids.

Vocabulary
according to

1 Classifying Materials

Teaching Activities

The purpose of this activity is to assess the pupils' existing knowledge which can then be built on throughout the unit.

Start by providing a selection of solid materials (at this stage all in 'lump' form) and ask the pupils to decide how they could sort them into two groups. They should be familiar with a number of simple properties that can be used for grouping, e.g. appearance, texture, transparency, magnetic properties. Encourage them to use these particular words, especially the word 'property'. Change the selection of materials a number of times to encourage the pupils to look for new groupings.

Introduce some liquids to the selection, and prompt the pupils to classify the materials into solids and liquids. Ask:

> Which materials are solids?
> Which materials are liquids?

Make sure the collection of materials includes some solids in lump form, and some liquids, coloured and colourless. Ask the pupils:

> What are the differences between solids and liquids?

Try to draw out the idea that solids have a fixed shape whereas liquids take up the shape of the container they are in. (This idea can be emphasised by having water in two different-shaped bottles showing how the water takes up different shapes.)

As the pupils become more familiar with the solid/liquid classification, introduce some crystals (sand and salt) and powders (flour). Ask:

> Are these solids or liquids?

The crystals and powders are obviously solids but they flow like liquids and, if the container is shaken, they take up the shape of the container.

Having checked the pupils' understanding of what a solid is, show them how a powder or crystals can be made from a lump – a sugar lump will do this well.

Pupil Consolidation

Ask the pupils to work in groups to make a list of all the liquids they come across at home. Compile the lists into one class list for display.

Ask the pupils to write down two differences between solids and liquids.

32

4D Solids and Liquids

2 Changing Solids to Liquids

Teaching Activities

Light a candle and leave it to burn for a short time. Ask the pupils:

> What is the candle made of? (wax)
> What is the wick made of? (string or cord)
> What is the liquid which forms around the wick whilst the candle is burning? (liquid wax)
> Where has this liquid come from? (the wax melts)
> What has made the liquid form? (heat from the flame)

Encourage the pupils to see the link between the heat from the flame and the melting of the candle wax. Emphasise the word 'melting'. Ask:

> What happens when this liquid is poured onto a piece of card?
> Why does it change back to a solid?
> What are the 'lumps' that are forming on the side of the candle?

Make sure the pupils understand the link between the changes in the wax and the temperature change.

Summarise that the candle wax has melted with the heat from the flame and formed liquid wax. When this hot liquid cools down it changes back to a solid. This second change is called freezing. The use of 'freezing' in this context may confuse the pupils. They will associate freezing with deep freezers and cold weather! 'Solidifying' is an alternative term but arguably is just as difficult. At this stage it is better not to mention the process unless pupils ask. Instead just refer to the liquid turning into a solid.

Organise the pupils in groups and then set them the following challenge:

> You will all be given an ice cube of the same size. Your task is to decide the best place in the classroom to put it so that it will melt the quickest.

You may wish to restrict the choice of places but give suggestions which might seem attractive, e.g. in a drawer in the dark, etc. Ask the groups to discuss their ideas for a few minutes before providing each with an ice cube in a container. You will need to allow at least 20 minutes before observations can be collected and compared. It may be appropriate for pupils to check their ice cube every five minutes. You could then produce a class bar chart showing the time taken to melt plotted against different places in the room.

Pupil Consolidation

Provide each group of pupils with a thermometer and ask them to measure the temperature of three given parts of the room. Suggest places where temperatures are significantly different, e.g. in a cool bag/fridge (about 5°C), on the window sill (about 20°C) and radiator (about 35°C). Give the groups three equal-sized ice cubes and ask them to find out how temperature affects how quickly the ice melts. Photocopiable master 4D PM2 can be used.

Timing
2 hours

Resources
- a large candle suitable for a demonstration
- sand tray to stand the candle in
- matches
- piece of card
- ice cubes in cold box or fridge
- small plastic trays or dishes
- thermometers
- stopwatch
- prepared results table and grid

Key words

(freezing)	melting
liquid	solid

Safety
Make sure the ice cubes can be placed safely on the radiator top or close to the radiator.

Pupil materials

Photocopiable master
Pupils measure how long it takes an ice cube to melt in three different places.

Pupil's Book pages 28 and 29
Prompted by photographs, pupils answer questions about melting.

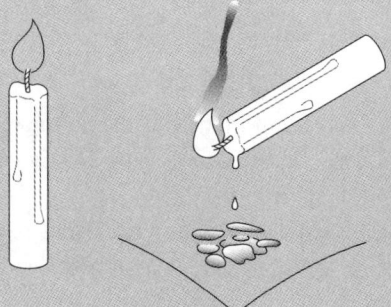

4D Solids and Liquids

3 Adding Solids to Water: Dissolving

Teaching Activities

Ask the pupils what they think happens when salt is added to water. Demonstrate by adding a spoonful of salt to some water in a transparent plastic cup. Introduce the word 'dissolve' rather than the word 'disappear' which the pupils are likely to use. Ask:

> Does the same thing happen when sand is added to water?

Try it – and show that the sand does not dissolve.

Provide groups of pupils with a range of solids to test (see Resources list). Ask them to add one measure of each solid to a fixed measure of water in a plastic cup and then stir the mixture for one minute. Ask:

> Can you still see any solid at the bottom of the cup?
> Can you see any solid floating in the liquid?
> Has the solid dissolved?

Prompt the pupils to repeat the exercise with all the solids and to show the results in a table. Table headings could be 'Solids which dissolve', 'Solids which do not dissolve'.

Explain that when a solid dissolves it mixes with the water and forms a solution. In a solution the particles of solid are broken down to a very small size and surrounded by water and so cannot be seen.

Pupil Consolidation

Ask the pupils:

> When salt has dissolved in water can we get it back?
> How might this be done?

Discuss whether the holes in a range of colanders and sieves would be small enough to 'catch' the small bits of salt. Introduce the filter paper, explaining that it has very small holes in it. Show the class how to fold the paper and put it in a funnel. Ask:

> Will the holes let the water through?
> Do you think the holes will catch the pieces of salt?

Attempt to filter the salt water, showing that the filter paper does not, in fact, help separate the salt from the water.

Ask the pupils what else they could try to 'get rid' of the water. Ask:

> How could you 'get rid' of the water?
> How do you remove water from wet clothes?
> How does a tumble drier get clothes dry?

Provide them with a small amount of salt solution (about 10cm³) to pour into a flat dish, saucer or transparent plastic cup and to leave in a warm place. An hour or so later, ask the pupils to explain what has happened. They should see that crystals of salt have formed around the edge of the cup. Evaporation is dealt with in detail in Year 5 (Units 5C and 5D), but you might like to mention the term here.

Timing
1½ hours

Resources
- transparent plastic cups
- small spoons
- a range of solids which dissolve (salt, sugar, alum) and a range of solids which do not dissolve (sand, soil, flour)
- a means of collecting and disposing of dirty water
- colanders and sieves
- filter paper
- funnels
- salt water
- flat dishes or saucers

Key words
dissolve filter
(evaporation) solution

Pupil materials

4D 30 Pupil's Book pages 30 and 31
4D 31 Prompted by photographs, pupils answer questions about dissolving.

34

4D Solids and Liquids

4 Which is the Best Filter?

Teaching Activities

The pupils should now understand that a solution (a solid dissolved in a liquid) cannot be separated into its components by filtering. Filtering can be used as a means of separating a solid from water only when the solid has not dissolved. Hold up a piece of filter paper and ask:

> Will this separate lumps of soil from dirty water?
> Will this separate sugar from lemonade?
> When can you use a filter to separate a mixture?

Provide the pupils with a range of possible materials for use as filters. Ask them to examine each item using a hand lens, to predict which material will make the best filter and to give a reason for their prediction. Ask:

> Will this material make a good filter?
> What can you see when you look at it with a hand lens?
> Which material will make the best filter?
> Why have you chosen this material?

Make up some chalk and water mixture and ask the pupils to find out which material acts as the best filter. (Chalk and water mixture works well as the 'whiteness' of the liquid which passes through the filter will clearly indicate which filter was the best.) Ask:

> Which filter will remove the most chalk from the water?
> Which filter will remove most of the white colour?

Encourage the pupils to consider how they will make sure that their test is fair. For example, always add the same amount of chalk/water; always shake the mixture before pouring it into the filter; use the same amount of filter material.

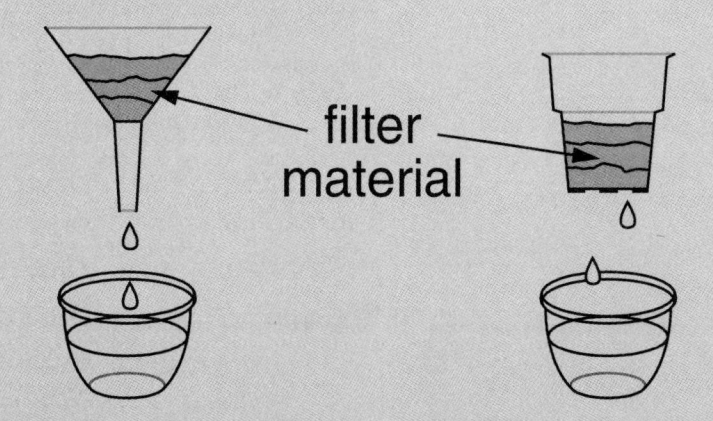

Pupil Consolidation

Ask the pupils to compare two or more different makes of coffee filter bags. Can they find out which is the best filter bag? They could use the chalk and water mixture again or a mixture made from ground coffee (not instant) and water.

Timing
2 hours

Resources
- filter funnels or yoghurt pots with holes in the bottom
- plastic cups
- materials for use as filters (muslin, cotton wool, paper towels) – include some which would not be suitable (plastic, aluminium foil)
- chalk/water mixture
- coffee filters (bleached and unbleached)

Key words
dissolve   solid
filter   solution

Pupil materials
4D 32 Pupil's Book pages 32 and 33
4D 33 Prompted by drawings of different types of filters, pupils answer questions about filtering.

Vocabulary
process
purify

4D Solids and Liquids

5 Separating the Mixture

Teaching Activities

This activity aims to consolidate some of the ideas encountered in the previous two activities i.e.

- a filter contains holes which let some materials through them but not others;
- filters will separate solid pieces from a mixture of solid and liquid;
- filters will not separate a solid from a liquid if the solid has dissolved and formed a solution;
- a liquid can be separated from the solid in a solution by evaporation.

Show the pupils unmixed samples of pea shingle, sand and salt so that they can see the separate components clearly. The pupils should work in groups. Give each group about $\frac{1}{3}$ of a cup-full of the mixture. If they need any further prompts show them some of the equipment they might use. Ask:

> Look at the mixture. What can you see?
> How would you separate the parts of the mixture?
> What could you remove first?
> What is the easiest part to remove?
> How could you remove the pea shingle?
> How could you remove the sand from the salt?

The pupils could pick out the pebbles, although a sieve will do the job much quicker. However, even a fine sieve will not separate sand and salt, so the pupils will need to add water and use a filter to do this.

Pupil Consolidation

Ask the pupils if they can remember how to get the salt back from the salt water (solution). They may have done this in Activity 3 or they could evaporate away the water in this activity. Alternatively, evaporation could be left to Year 5.

Timing
2 hours

Resources
- pea shingle, sand and salt as individual components and as a mixture
- sieves of various sizes
- plastic cups
- filter funnels or yoghurt pots
- suitable filter material (filter paper or cotton wool)
- spoons

Key words

(evaporate)   mixture
filter   sieve

4D Solids and Liquids

6 Key Activity: Investigating Dissolving

Timing
2 hours

Resources
- sugar, salt, alum (from a pharmacist)
- measuring cylinders
- spoons
- transparent plastic containers

Key words
dissolve   solution

Pupil materials

4D PM3 — Photocopiable master
Pupils use a writing frame to guide their investigation of dissolving.

Previous Experience
The pupils should have:

- sorted solids into those that dissolve and those that do not dissolve in water;
- used a measuring cylinder to measure volume;
- used tables to present results;
- used bar charts to display their results.

Knowing that there is a limit to how much of a solid can be dissolved in a fixed amount of liquid is beyond the scope of the current National Curriculum programme of study. However, the pupils should be able to undertake this investigation successfully without needing to explain why no more solid will dissolve.

Set the questions for the investigation:

> How much of a solid can you dissolve in 30 ml of water at room temperature?
>
> Does the amount that dissolves depend on which solid you use?

Start with a general introduction. To answer the above questions, the pupils will be comparing at least two solids which dissolve in water. Look at the solids together (sugar, salt and alum) and then ask the pupils how they can make sure they test each of the solids in the same way. Ask:

> What will you use to measure out the solid?
>
> Is stirring important?
>
> How will you know when no more solid can dissolve?

Show the pupils the range of equipment they can use for the investigation.

Hand out Photocopiable master 4DPM3 and ask the pupils to complete the first section on their own.

They can then carry out the investigation in small groups, recording their result for each solid in the space given on the photocopiable master. Encourage them to complete the master and, if possible, produce a bar chart to summarise their results.

Assessment

The Assessment Pointers for Sc1 illustrate the possible levels of attainment in the context of the Key Activity.

Assessment Pointers for Sc1

Level	Planning Pupils can:	Obtaining and Presenting Pupils can:	Considering and Evaluating Pupils can:
2	make suggestions, with prompting, as to how the amount of solid that dissolves can be measured;	show the results in a simple table giving the name of the solid and how many 'measures' mixed with the water;	compare findings with expectations e.g. 'I thought the salt would be best not the sugar'.
3	put forward ideas, e.g. 'all the solids a spoonful at a time until no more dissolves';	use a spoon or scoop to measure out carefully equal quantities of solid;	write a conclusion such as 'the sugar dissolved the best, salt was second best'.
4	plan a test which uses the same amount of water for each solid, and uses the same spoon to measure out each solid;	produce a simple bar chart showing the amount dissolved for each solid;	suggest simple improvements e.g. 'it would have been better if I had kept the spoon dry as some sugar stuck to the spoon'.

Pupil materials

4D PM4

End of Unit Question
Photocopiable master
Pupils answer questions about different liquids and draw a bar chart.

Mark Scheme

Question	Answers
1	treacle
2	between 3–9 seconds
3	one drop of each, same distance of 'run'
4	bar chart completed correctly – bars in correct heights, correct labels

The Assessment Pointers for Sc3 illustrate how evidence from responses to questions and tasks in the Pupil's Book and on the Photocopiable masters can be related to the different levels of attainment.

Assessment Pointers for Sc3

Level	Evidence	Typical Outcome Pupils can:
2	Solids and Liquids – Pupil's Book page 27 q.2	identify three liquids;
	Solids and Liquids in the Home – 4DPM1	name at least three solids and three liquids.
3	Changing Solids into Liquids – Pupil's Book page 29 qs. 1, 2, 4	talk or write about melting in the context of a burning candle;
	Dissolving – Pupil's Book page 31 qs.1, 2, 3	name two solids which dissolve in water and at least one that does not; name an example of a solution.
4	Filters and Filtering – Pupil's Book page 33 q. 3	give a reason why filtering will not separate a dissolved solid from a solution.

4E Friction

⏱ **Timing**
11 hours

Key Ideas for Teachers

Forces are measured in newtons using a forcemeter or a newtonmeter. A force of 1 N will lift a 100 g mass against the force of gravity.

Friction is a force that exists between two surfaces as they try to rub past each other. The origin of the force can be visualised if you imagine two solid surfaces greatly magnified – the surfaces will be far from smooth, and peaks and troughs on one surface can interlock with troughs and peaks on the other surface. In order for the surfaces to move over each other force must be used to disturb the interlocking. Once moving, the force needed to maintain motion is usually less than that needed initially to start movement. This is because the peaks and troughs on the surfaces cannot successfully interlock once motion has been achieved.

Friction can be a very useful force – bicycles and cars depend on their tyres providing friction as they move across the road surface, as do most shoes that we wear. However, friction between moving parts in motors or engines can be very wasteful. Energy is transferred into 'useless' heat and sometimes sound. Lubricants are therefore used extensively to reduce friction.

Air resistance and water resistance are both forms of friction. Objects are streamlined to reduce frictional forces, e.g. cars, racing cycle helmets, etc. However, air resistance is very useful e.g. to a skydiver, when spreading the body creates more air resistance and so reduces the speed of descent.

Glossary of terms

air resistance	the frictional force that exists between an object and the air it is moving through
friction	the force that exists between two surfaces or substances
gravity	a force that pulls everything towards the centre of the Earth
streamlining	changing the shape of an object to reduce air or water resistance
water resistance	the frictional force resistance that exists between an object and the water it is moving through

Key Ideas for Pupils

- objects are pulled downwards because of the gravitational attraction between them and the Earth;
- friction, including air resistance, is a force which slows moving objects and may prevent objects from starting to move;
- forces can be measured and the direction in which they act identified.

These learning outcomes illustrate how the key ideas for pupils can be matched to different levels of attainment. They can also be used to check the level of demand of an activity.

Starting points

Pupils should be familiar with the following ideas:
- that forces can cause things to get faster, slow down or change direction;
- that both pushes and pulls are examples of forces;
- friction is a force.

Learning Outcomes

Pupils can:

Level 2	• describe some ways in which friction can be increased and some ways in which friction can be decreased;	• identify friction as a force; • compare the grip of two different shoes.
Level 3	• describe some of the factors that increase friction between solid surfaces and increase air and water resistance;	• describe how to measure forces using a newtonmeter; • make simple conclusions from experimental results.
Level 4	• describe situations where frictional forces are useful as well as situations where frictional forces cause problems;	• support a conclusion using knowledge about friction.

The Assessment Pointers on page 46 show how these levels of attainment can be interpreted in the context of the specific activities used in the unit.

4E Friction

⏱ Timing
1½ hours

✏ Resources
- sugar paper
- pens/crayons

Key words
air resistance	push
force	rough
friction	smooth
gravity	squeeze
newton	streamlining
pull	twist

Pupil materials
4E PM1 Photocopiable master. Pupils identify different friction forces on a drawing of a playground.

1 Forces All Around

Teaching Activities
The purpose of this activity is to reinforce the pupils' memory of forces and to introduce friction.

Ask the pupils to work in groups to create a concept map. Start with 'Forces' in the middle and ask the pupils to include what they know about the different types of forces and what they do. The sort of things they might include are:

- types of force: push, pull, twist, stretch, squash, gravity, friction;
- what forces do: speed things up, slow things down, change the direction;
- how forces are measured: forcemeter, newtons, newtonmeter.

Give the pupils the following words and ask them to include these on the concept maps (this is more difficult as they may be unfamiliar with these terms):

- grip, air resistance, streamlining

Ask some of the groups to show and explain their concept maps. Explain some of the ideas they are not familiar with.

Ask questions, such as:

> What is air resistance? (the air pushing against something)
> Who can give me an example of where air resistance is important? (parachute)
> Has anyone heard of streamlining?
> What is a streamlined shape? Can you give an example? (a fast car or aeroplane)
> Why are things streamlined? (to reduce air resistance)

Pupil Consolidation
Provide the pupils with Photocopiable master 4EPM1. Ask them to look at the drawing of a park and to circle where there are friction forces.

Suggest pupils write a short story about living in a world with no friction. You might like to provide some clues first (no grip, no air resistance) and discuss these.

4E Friction

2 Measuring Forces

Teaching Activities

Remind the pupils that forces can be measured with a forcemeter, known as a newtonmeter, and that force is measured in newtons. Show the pupils a newtonmeter and explain that it contains a spring that stretches when a force pulls on it.

Ask:

❝ How big do you think a force of 1 newton is?

How many newtons of force do you think would be needed to lift this bean bag? ❞

Demonstrate the use of the newtonmeter to lift a few objects, asking the pupils to make a prediction each time. Prompt individual pupils to come to the front of the class and lift the object.

Explain that friction is a force that occurs between two surfaces.

Set the task: the pupils will be pulling a margarine tub containing different masses across different surfaces and measuring the force needed. They should use three different masses on each surface. Encourage the pupils to make and record their predictions (using Photocopiable master 4EPM2) before taking the measurement.

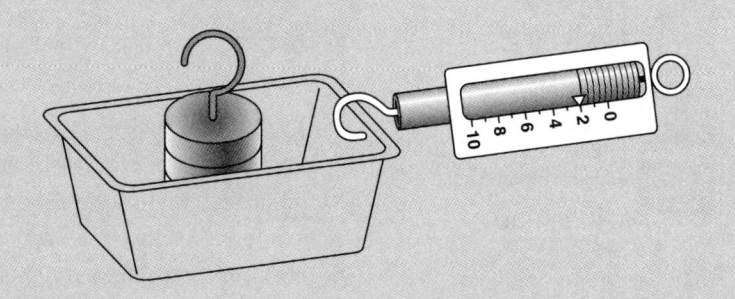

After making their measurements the pupils should be able to answer the following questions:

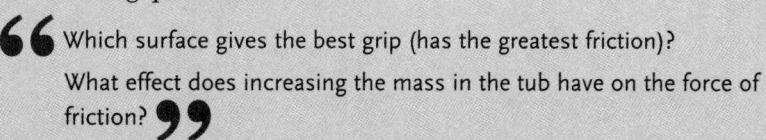

❝ Which surface gives the best grip (has the greatest friction)?

What effect does increasing the mass in the tub have on the force of friction? ❞

The first question is similar to one included in Unit 2E, Activity 4:

❝ How slippery is the floor? ❞

If the pupils have not covered this activity before it does provide a good context for measuring forces (i.e. safety in school).

Pupil Consolidation

Suggest the pupils try to make their own force measurers using rubber bands. For example, they could use a rubber band fastened at one end to the top of a piece of dowel. Can they add a scale marked in newtons? (Marks can be made on the dowel.)

Timing
1½ hours

Resources
- margarine tubs
- an assortment of different masses
- newtonmeters
- access to different surfaces (wood, plastic tiles, carpet, concrete, tarmac, grass)
- rubber bands

Key words
friction   newtonmeter
newton   surface

Pupil materials

4E PM2 Photocopiable master
Pupils compare the friction on different surfaces.

4E Friction

Timing
2 hours

Resources
- a bicycle
- trays or other suitable surfaces
- margarine tubs
- various masses
- newtonmeters
- a range of lubricants (water, butter or margarine, tomato sauce, cooking oil)
- graph paper

Key words
friction   newtonmeter
lubricant

Pupil materials

4E 34 / 4E 35 — Pupil's Book pages 34 and 35 Prompted by photographs, pupils identify situations where friction forces exist.

3 Reducing Friction

Teaching Activities

Ask the pupils:

" What would happen if there was no friction between your shoes and the ground?

What would happen if there was no friction between bicycle brake blocks and the wheel rims? "

Use a bicycle to illustrate to the class all the places where friction is important, e.g. grips on handlebars, seat, pads on pedals, brake pads, tyres, etc. Ask the pupils to make a list of situations where friction is useful.

Ask:

" Can you think of times when friction is a nuisance? (e.g. when pulling a sledge, when pulling something across the floor, etc.) "

Use the bicycle again to illustrate all the places where friction would be a nuisance, e.g. on the chain, in the bearings on the pedal and handlebars, etc. Again, ask the pupils to make a list.

Introduce the idea of lubrication by asking:

" How can we reduce the amount of friction on a bicycle? "

Discuss the pupils' responses. Possible responses include: using oil or grease.

Organise an investigation where the pupils look at a number of lubricants to find out which is the most effective, i.e. reduces friction the most. The investigation could be carried out as a class practical, or it may be more manageable as a demonstration. Take a measurement first using no lubricant for comparison purposes. Spread the lubricant on a flat surface, e.g. a tray, and then pull a loaded margarine tub across the surface. Possible lubricants include water, butter or margarine, tomato sauce, cooking oil. Encourage the pupils to discuss the results and draw conclusions. Ask:

" Which was the best lubricant?

How could you tell from your results? "

Pupil Consolidation

Draw a bar chart to show the results of the experiment.

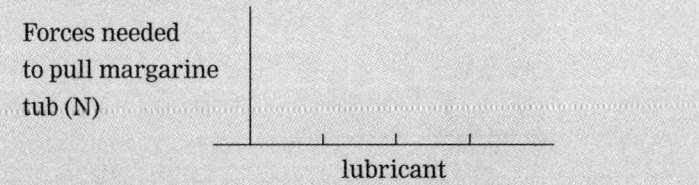

Forces needed
to pull margarine
tub (N)

lubricant

Explain that water *does* reduce friction. Ask the pupils whether water would be a good lubricant to use on a bicycle, and to explain their answer. Hopefully the pupils will know that water helps metal (iron or steel) to rust whereas oil stops rusting.

4E Friction

4 Streamlining

Teaching Activities

Use photographs or pictures to illustrate examples of streamlining. Include examples of streamlining for travel through air as well as through water. Ask the pupils why they think streamlining is important. Ask:

> Why are trains streamlined?
> Why do racing cyclists wear helmets that are pointed?
> Why are boats pointed at the front?

Divide the class into groups. Give each group a mass of plasticene of the same size and a measuring cylinder or transparent tube filled with water. The pupils can investigate which shapes are the most streamlined by producing different shapes from the plasticene and dropping them into the tube or cylinder containing water. The time it takes for the plasticene to fall to the bottom of the tube can be used as a measure of the effectiveness of the streamlining. The longer the tube or cylinder, the easier it will be to measure accurately the time taken. They should try and test about five different shapes.

Ask:

> Which shape sank the quickest?
> Which shape sank the slowest?
> Which shape was the most streamlined?

To ensure a fair test it is important to use the same piece of plasticene each time. Consequently, either the cylinder will need to be emptied and filled between tests or a thread of cotton could be attached to the shape before it is dropped, thus enabling it to be pulled out of the water. The pupils should use Photocopiable master 4EPM3 to record their results and to draw a conclusion.

It is important to emphasise that the plasticene falls due to the force of gravity and that this can be shown on a drawing as an arrow pointing vertically downwards from the plasticene. The water resistance is a force which can be shown as an arrow pointing vertically upwards from the plasticene. The pupils should be familiar with using arrows to represent forces.

Pupil Consolidation

Ask the pupils to list four objects that are streamlined to reduce air resistance, and four objects that are streamlined to reduce water resistance, e.g. air resistance – rocket, aeroplane, javelin, etc. water resistance – torpedo, submarine, yacht, swimmer (with costume), etc.

Timing
2 hours

Resources
- plasticene
- long transparent tubes or measuring cylinders
- cotton thread
- stopwatches

Key words
friction   water resistance
streamlined

Pupil materials

4E PM3 Photocopiable master
Pupils try to find the most streamlined shape in water.

4E 36
4E 37 Pupil's Book pages 36 and 37
Prompted by photographs, pupils answer questions about streamlining.

Vocabulary
designed

ICT Opportunity
opportunity for research

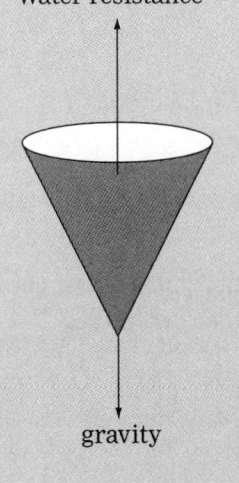

4E Friction

Timing
2 hours

Resources
- parachute material (fabric or plastic)
- cotton
- scissors
- a 'parachutist' (plastic figure or plasticene)
- cake/bun cases
- stopwatches

Key words
air resistance   parachute
gravity

Pupil materials

4E 38 Pupil's Book pages 38 and 39
4E 39 Pupils answer questions about parachutes and air resistance.

Vocabulary
caused by
free-fall

5 Parachutes

Teaching Activities

This activity considers the factors affecting air resistance in a little more detail.

The pupils can investigate how the size of a parachute affects how quickly it falls. The parachute can be made simply by attaching cotton from the four corners of a piece of plastic or fabric to a central figure, or lump of plasticene.

However, there are two difficulties with this activity. Firstly, the cotton gets tangled easily and some pupils lack the skill, or indeed the patience, to construct the parachutes successfully. Secondly, a significant drop of at least 2 m is needed to time the fall. An alternative method is to use cake/bun cases which drop remarkably slowly making timing over smaller distances feasible. The size of the 'parachute' can be changed by flattening out the cake case. This will change significantly the time of descent.

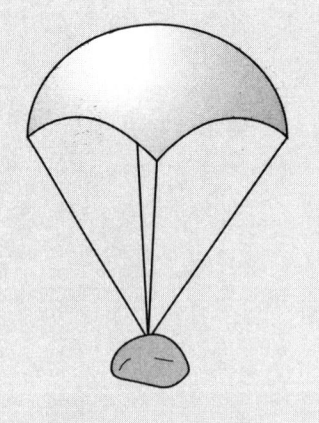

The pupils should be encouraged to make predictions and support them with scientific understanding, e.g. the bigger the parachute the slower it will fall because the air resistance will be greater. Ask:

> Which parachute will fall the slowest?
> Why do you think it will fall the slowest?

The pupils should also be able to label a drawing of their parachute falling with arrows to represent gravity and air resistance, showing that these forces act in opposite directions.

Pupil Consolidation

Prompt the pupils to draw a diagram of a parachutist drifting towards the ground, using arrows to label gravity and air resistance.

Ask the pupils to explain why a parachutist with a larger parachute will fall more slowly than one with a smaller parachute.

4E Friction

6 Key Activity: Which Shoes Give the Best Grip?

Previous Experience
The pupils will need to:
- have used a newtonmeter to measure force;
- know that friction is a force and that good grip means a large friction force;
- have compared the grip offered by different surfaces.

The pupils will need to compare at least three or four different shoes to see which has the best grip. This can be done by pulling the shoes over the same surface and measuring the force needed to do this. Ask the pupils questions such as:

> How could you test different shoes to see which has the best grip? What would you need to measure?
> How can you make your test fair?

Give the pupils a chance to try their approach with one of their own shoes. They may need to put a fixed mass in the shoe in order to get measurable readings. Ask the pupils to consider whether they will measure the force needed to start the shoe moving, or the force needed to keep it moving. (In fact, it doesn't matter which so long as they are consistent in their approach.)

The pupils should complete the Planning section of Photocopiable master 4EPM4 before undertaking the investigation with different shoes. Encourage them to take each reading a few times until they are satisfied that they have an accurate reading. Results and conclusions should be included on the Photocopiable master and a bar chart produced to summarise the results.

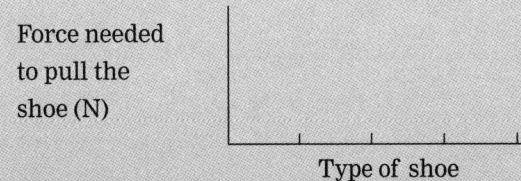

Timing
2 hours

Resources
- an assortment of masses
- newtonmeters
- access to different shoes

Key words
fair test   grip
friction

Pupil materials

4E PM4 Photocopiable master
Pupils use a writing frame to guide their investigation of the grip provided by different types of shoe.

4E 40 **4E 41** Pupil's Book pages 40 and 41
Prompted by photographs, pupils compare the grip obtained from different types of shoe.

Force needed to pull the shoe (N)

Type of shoe

Assessment

The Assessment Pointers for Sc1 illustrate the possible levels of attainment in the context of the Key Activity.

Assessment Pointers for Sc1

Level	Planning Pupils can:	Obtaining and Presenting Pupils can:	Considering and Evaluating Pupils can:
2	with help, decide how they can test the shoes;	compare what happened with different shoes on the same surface, e.g. 'this shoe was harder to pull than that one';	compare findings with expectations, e.g. 'I was right, Jane's shoe had the most grip'.
3	make suggestions as to how the grip of different shoes can be compared;	use the newtonmeter to measure accurately the force needed to pull each shoe;	provide a simple conclusion, e.g. 'Jane's trainer had the best grip because it took the largest force to move it'.
4	make simple predictions, such as 'I think this trainer will have the most grip because it has lots of grooves';	take each reading several times to ensure that they have an accurate reading;	link a conclusion to their knowledge of friction, e.g. 'Jane's trainer was the best because more of it was touching the ground'.

Pupil materials

4E PM5
End of Unit Question
Photocopiable master
Pupils answer questions about the grip obtained from different shoes.

Mark Scheme

Question	Answers
1	arrow pointing towards the pulley
2	gravity
3	friction
4	the one with the best grip needs the greatest weight

The Assessment Pointers for Sc4 illustrate how evidence from responses to questions and tasks in the Pupil's Book and on the Photocopiable masters can be related to the different levels of attainment.

Assessment Pointers for Sc4

Level	Evidence	Typical Outcome Pupils can:
2	Grip – Pupil's Book page 41 qs. 1, 2	select which trainer will give the best grip in dry and wet weather;
	Friction – 4EPM1	identify friction forces in a number of everyday situations.
3	Streamlining – Pupil's Book page 37 qs.1, 2, 3	show understanding of which shapes are streamlined and apply their ideas in the context of cars and swimmers;
	Streamlined shape– 4EPM3	talk or write about streamlining and water resistance.
4	Friction and Lubricants – Pupil's Book page 35 qs.1, 2, 3, 4	list ways of reducing friction in the context of cars, skiing and the use of lubricants; identify useful friction in the context of a bicycle;
	Forces – 4EPM5 q.4	interpret the results given, linking ideas on grip to friction.

4F Circuits and Conductors

Key Ideas for Teachers

Electricity will flow only through certain materials known as electrical conductors. Materials which resist the flow of electricity are known as insulators. Electrical conductors contain electrons which are free to move when connected in a circuit with a battery. The battery can be considered as an 'electron pump' – electrons are pushed around the circuit and travel through the conducting material.

The simplest way of combining components is in a series circuit. A series circuit is one in which there is only one route for the electrons to flow. This is in contrast to a parallel circuit in which the electrons have a choice of routes. Most of the circuits used in everyday devices are parallel circuits. In this unit parallel circuits are not specifically introduced through the main activities, although some pupils can be introduced to them via the consolidation activities.

The analogy of electricity flow and water flow is useful here. The cell or battery can be thought of as a 'pump', the larger the battery the greater the force or pressure (voltage) provided by the pump. When a cell is connected to a bulb with two connecting wires the bulb will be bright. If another bulb is put in the circuit both bulbs will be dimmer. This can be explained by imagining that the bulb acts as a constriction (resistance) in the circuit and slows down the rate of flow of the electrons. The more bulbs or components in the circuit the more constrictions and so the slower the rate of flow (the lower the current). Many components need a minimum current before they will work and these minima are different for different components. For example, if a motor and buzzer are connected in series one may work and the other may not! For them both to work in the circuit it may be necessary to connect them in parallel.

Key Ideas for Pupils

- construct circuits, including a battery or power supply and a range of switches, to make electrical devices work e.g. buzzers, motors;
- changing the number or type of components e.g. batteries, bulbs, wires in a series circuit can make bulbs brighter or dimmer.

These learning outcomes illustrate how the key ideas for pupils can be matched to different levels of attainment. They can also be used to check the level of demand of an activity.

Timing
10 hours

Glossary of terms

battery	an electrical source made by combining cells
cell	a simple source of electricity
circuit	an arrangement of wires and components
current	a flow of electrons in a circuit
parallel circuit	a circuit which provides more than one route for the current to flow
resistance	a measure of how much the current flow is restricted
series circuit	a circuit which provides a single route for the current to flow
voltage	a measure of the energy or 'push' provided to the electrons

Starting points

Pupils should be familiar with the following ideas:
- many common appliances use electricity, some from the mains, some from batteries;
- there are dangers associated with the use of mains electricity;
- a complete circuit is needed before the components in the circuit will work.

Learning Outcomes

Pupils can:

Level 2	distinguish between those common appliances that use batteries and those that use mains electricity;	construct and make drawings of simple circuits; explain why some circuits work and others do not; record measurements in a simple (provided) table.
Level 3	identify common electrical conductors and insulators;	construct circuits from circuit drawings, using switches as appropriate; identify patterns in results.
Level 4	explain why components in a series circuit need to be 'matched' if they are all to work;	use a bar chart to display results.

The Assessment Pointers on page 53 show how these levels of attainment can be interpreted in the context of the specific activities used in the unit.

4F Circuits and Conductors

1 Electrical Circuits

Teaching Activities

The pupils should be familiar with simple electrical circuits from their work in Unit 2F (Using Electricity). The purpose of this activity is to assess what they can remember and to use a basic model of electricity flow to help their understanding of simple circuits.

Show the pupils a portable/mains radio or CD player. Ask:

> Can you think of two ways of making the radio work?
> What is the best way to use it in this classroom?
> Which is the best way to use it in the garden at home?

Talk to the pupils about the advantages and disadvantages of mains and battery sources of electricity. Organise groups and ask them to think of four safety rules for using mains electricity. Produce a class list of rules to display in the classroom. (See example in margin.)

Show the pupils the wires/leads and components (cells, bulbs, motors, buzzers) that they will be using to make simple circuits. Ask them to name each of the components and to guess the purpose of each one in the circuit. Set the pupils a challenge to make:

- a circuit using a cell and one bulb so that the bulb lights up;
- another circuit using a cell so that two bulbs light up.

It will quickly become apparent how much additional guidance the pupils will need to make the two circuits successfully. It may be necessary to reinforce the need for a complete circuit. The pupils should notice a difference in the brightness of the bulbs in the two circuits. Can they explain why the brightness of the bulbs differs? An answer to this question can be given through the use of drama/role-play.

electricity (current)	pupils walking slowly round the circuit
a cell	a pupil who provides a gentle push to each 'electron' (pupil) as it passes
a bulb	a pupil sitting on a chair who raises both hands when touched on the shoulder by an 'electron'

You can model the following situations:

complete circuit	the electrons cannot move unless there is a route back to the cell/battery, i.e. no route back causes a 'traffic jam'
more cells	the electrons are given a bigger push and so have more energy and move more quickly
more bulbs	these tend to slow down the movement of the electrons and so each bulb gets less energy
short circuit	with no bulb in the circuit the electrons have nothing to pass their energy on to and so return and 'bump' into the cell/battery

---

Timing
2 hours

Resources
- portable radio or CD player
- plastic covered leads
- crocodile clips
- cells and holders
- bulbs and holders
- access to the school hall for role-play/drama

Key words
battery	circuit
bulb	electricity
cell	lead

Pupil materials

4F 42 Pupil's Book pages 42 and 43
4F 43 Pupils look at drawings of electrical circuits and identify components.

Vocabulary
return to

	Advantages	Disadvantages
Mains	easy to use	can not be used away from the supply, can be dangerous
Battery	can be used anywhere safe to use	they run out, can be expensive

4F Circuits and Conductors

2 Conductors and Insulators

Teaching Activities

Show the pupils a plastic covered lead, and ask them:

"What is inside the plastic covering for the electricity to pass through? What is the plastic covering for?"

Explain that an electrical conductor is a material that allows electricity to pass through it. A material which does not allow electricity to pass through it is called an insulator. Can the pupils test materials to see if they are conductors or insulators?

Show the pupils the sort of circuit that can be used and how they can test different materials in the circuit.

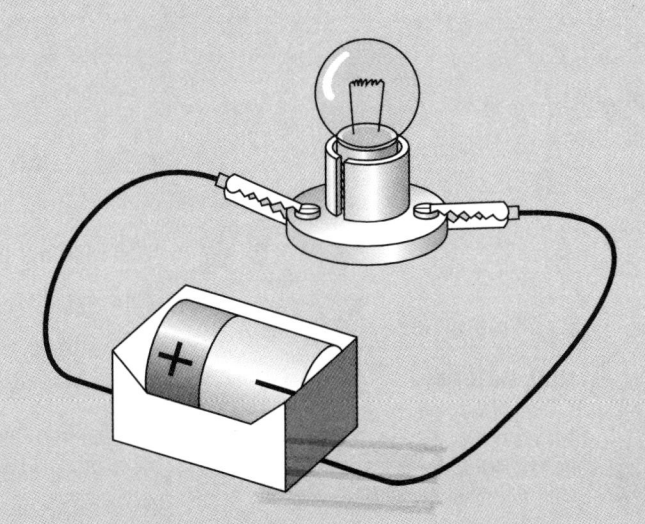

Show the pupils the collection of objects they will be testing in the circuit. Ask them to predict which objects will allow the electricity to pass through, i.e. are made from a conducting material, and which will not allow electricity to pass through, i.e. are made from an insulating material. The pupils can then work in groups and use Photocopiable master 4FPM1 to record their results.

Discuss each group's results as a class and identify the pattern: all metals are conductors and other materials are not. It might be better to leave out graphite, making the rule very easy to identify and use.

Pupil Consolidation

The pupils have just discovered that all metals are conductors of electricity. Do they think that all metals are magnetic? Note: Pupils often think that all metals are magnetic. In fact they are not. Only iron and steel of the common metals are magnetic.

Timing
2 hours

Resources
- a range of metallic (conducting) objects: scissors, beer bottle tops, nails, milk bottle tops, paper clips, tins, coins, etc.
- a range of non-metallic (insulating) objects: cork, plastic carton, paper bag, wooden spoon, fabric, etc.
- cells and holders
- plastic covered leads
- crocodile clips
- bulbs and holders

Key words
circuit   insulator
conductor

Pupil materials

4F PM1 Photocopiable master Pupils test different materials to see if they are electrical conductors.

4F 44 **4F 45** Pupil's Book pages 44 and 45 Prompted by photographs, pupils identify electrical insulators and conductors.

4F Circuits and Conductors

3 Switches

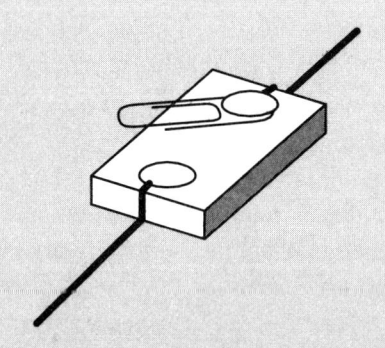

Teaching Activities

This activity is similar to one in Unit 2F. However, it is important that pupils can make a variety of switches to assemble different circuits containing a range of components, such as motors and buzzers.

Show the pupils some of the commercially produced switches that can be used later in their circuits. Ask questions such as:

> Why is it useful to use switches in circuits?
> How do switches work?

Show the pupils a simple aluminium foil 'fold switch' and ask them to make one to control a circuit.

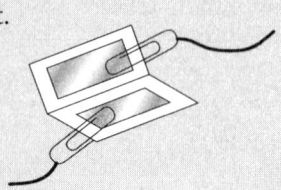

When the pupils have successfully made the foil switches ask them:

> Why is aluminium used in this switch?
> Could we use cling film instead?

Then ask the pupils to make another type of switch using split pins and a paper clip. When the task has been completed ask:

> Why is a paper clip used in this type of switch?
> Could we use a match stick instead of the paper clip?

Ask pupils to practise making different types of circuit using bulbs, motors and buzzers. They should be encouraged to draw the circuits they make, using Photocopiable master 4FPM2. They will have problems making all the components work in the same circuit. In many instances the components won't 'match' (that is, they have different voltage or current ratings). If, for example, two bulbs in a series circuit are of different brightness, prompt the pupils to look at the ratings printed on the side of the bulb.

Simple parallel circuits can be introduced if appropriate. It is best to make a series circuit with one component only and then to add the second component to the first circuit without disrupting the first circuit.

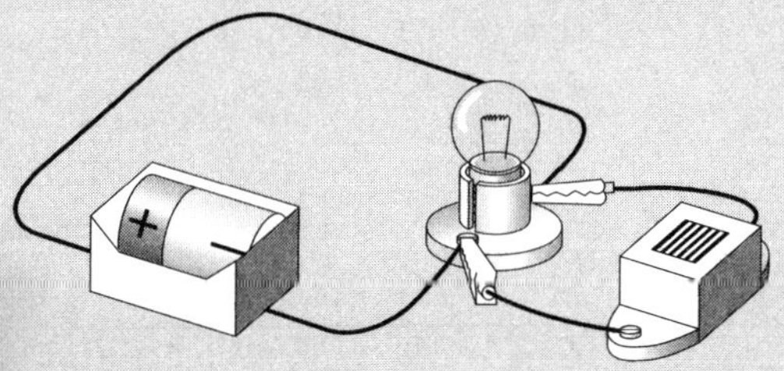

Pupil Consolidation

Suggest the pupils try to make a circuit containing two bulbs where the electricity has a choice of routes round the circuit. What do they notice about the brightness of the bulbs?

Timing
2 hours

Resources
- plastic covered leads
- crocodile clips
- cells and holders
- bulbs and holders
- motors
- buzzers
- aluminium foil
- split pins
- paper clips
- card

Key words
conductor   switch

Pupil materials

4F PM2 Photocopiable master Pupils draw and write about circuits they have made.

4F 46 **4F 47** Pupil's Book pages 46 and 47 Prompted by drawings and photographs, pupils answer questions about switches.

Vocabulary
devices

4F Circuits and Conductors

4 Making Use of Electricity

Teaching Activities

This activity provides an opportunity for the pupils to put their understanding of circuits into action by making some electrical items. It may be necessary to allocate different items to different groups of pupils to match different levels of ability.

It is also an opportunity to introduce the use of LEDs (light emitting diodes). LEDs will only work if connected in a circuit the 'right way round', in the same way that buzzers will only work if connected the right way round.

The suggested activities are:

Item	Circuit	Notes
Steady Hand Game	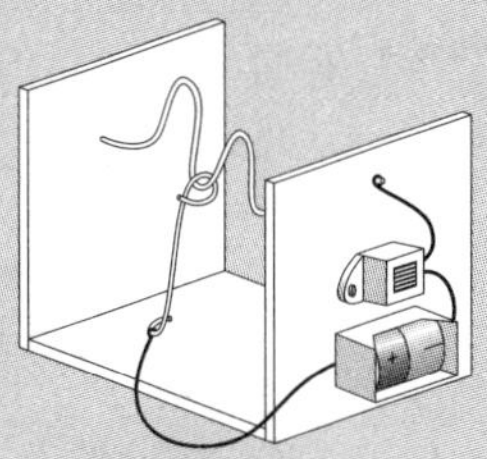	series circuit with cell and buzzer
Lighthouse	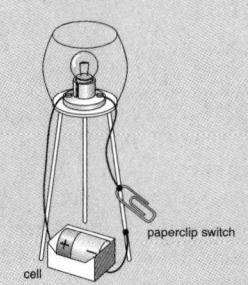	series circuit with cell and bulb
Quiz Game	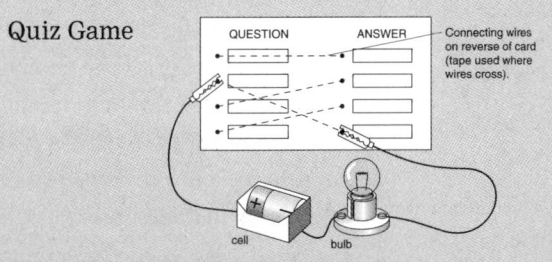	a number of series circuits with cells and buzzer
Christmas Tree Card		a parallel circuit with cell, switch and LEDs

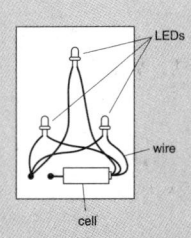

When the pupils have completed their items encourage them to talk about the circuit they have used and how it works. Ask:

" How does your game/card/lighthouse work?
How have you made your circuit?
What problems did you have? "

Timing
2 hours

Resources
- cells and holders
- wires
- bulbs and holders
- motors
- LEDs
- crocodile clips
- masking tape
- split pins
- thick wire
- card
- scissors

Key words
circuit　　　　series circuit
parallel circuit

4F Circuits and Conductors

5 Key Activity: What Affects the Brightness of a Bulb?

Timing
2 hours

Resources
- 1.5V cells
- cells and holders or masking tape
- bulbs and holders
- plastic coated wire
- crocodile clips
- paper tissues

Key words
battery   cell
brightness   circuit

Pupil materials

4F PM3 — Photocopiable master. Pupils use a writing frame to guide their investigation of the brightness of a bulb.

4F 48 — Pupil's Book page 48. Prompted by drawings, pupils answer questions about circuits.

Vocabulary
dim

Previous Experience
The pupils should have:

- made simple circuits;
- made predictions and supported them with scientific knowledge;
- used bar charts to represent results.

The pupils will now be aware that when more than one bulb is used in a circuit the bulbs are not very bright. Show them a series circuit with one cell and two bulbs in it. Ask:

Why are the bulbs so dim?
How could you make them brighter?

Suggestions might include taking one bulb out of the circuit altogether, or even using a parallel circuit. Both suggestions would work. Remember that pupils do *not* need to be familiar with parallel circuits.

Explain the investigation: the pupils will be exploring what happens to the brightness of the bulbs when more cells are added to the circuit, and considering how they might measure the brightness. Suggest that one way is to cover the bulb with layers of tissue paper and to add layers until the light from the bulb can no longer be seen. Ask:

How could we measure the brightness of the bulbs?
Do we need to measure the brightness of both bulbs?
Does it matter which bulb brightness we measure?

Organise the pupils into groups. Provide them with copies of Photocopiable master 4FPM3 which they should use to predict how the brightness of the bulb depends on how many cells are in the circuit. They should use two bulbs throughout but need only to measure the brightness of one bulb (the same) each time. The pupils should try one, two and three cells in the circuit and note the effects. It is unlikely that they will be able to use four cells without blowing the bulbs, but this does depend on how new the cells are. You might like to try this out before the lesson so that you can suggest a safe upper limit on the number of cells to be used. After the investigation the pupils should complete the Photocopiable master and draw a bar chart to show their results.

Assessment

The Assessment Pointers for Sc1 illustrate the possible levels of attainment in the context of the Key Activity.

Assessment Pointers for Sc1

Level	Planning Pupils can:	Obtaining and Presenting Pupils can:	Considering and Evaluating Pupils can:
2	make suggestions as to how the brightness of the bulbs can be changed;	record measurements in a simple table;	compare findings with expectations, e.g. 'I thought the bulb would be brighter with more batteries!'.
3	make suggestions as to how the brightness of the bulbs can be compared;	use the tissue paper in layers to obtain a measure of the brightness of the bulb;	identify a pattern in the results such as 'the more cells there were the brighter the bulb was'.
4	make predictions such as 'the more cells there are the brighter the bulb will be because there will be more electricity';	produce a bar chart showing how the number of cells alters the brightness of the bulb;	Link their conclusions to scientific ideas, e.g. 'the bulb was brighter with more cells because there was more electricity'.

Pupil materials

4F PM4 End of Unit Question Photocopiable master
Pupils identify electrical conductors and insulators and explain why a circuit will not work.

Mark Scheme

Question	Answers
1	plastic comb, wooden spoon (bulb does not light) aluminium foil (bulb does light)
2	the cells are incorrectly connected (positive to positive)

The Assessment Pointers for Sc4 illustrate how evidence from responses to questions and tasks in the Pupil's Book and on the Photocopiable masters can be related to the different levels of attainment.

Assessment Pointers for Sc4

Level	Evidence	Typical Outcome Pupils can:
2	Electrical Circuits – Pupil's Book page 43 qs.1, 2	identify three things which use mains electricity and three things which use electricity from batteries;
	Making Circuits – 4FPM2	draw some of the circuits they have made.
3	Electrical Conductors and Insulators – Pupil's Book page 45 qs. 1, 2, 3, 4	name examples of electrical conductors and insulators and explain, for example, why plastic is used as a coating for electrical wires;
	Circuits – 4FPM4 q.1	identify aluminium as the only object which will light the bulb, i.e. as an electrical conductor.
4	Unusual Circuits – Pupil's Book page 48	identify the difference between the two bulbs and explain why this might cause a problem in a circuit.

The Human Skeleton

4A PM1

This is a human skeleton.

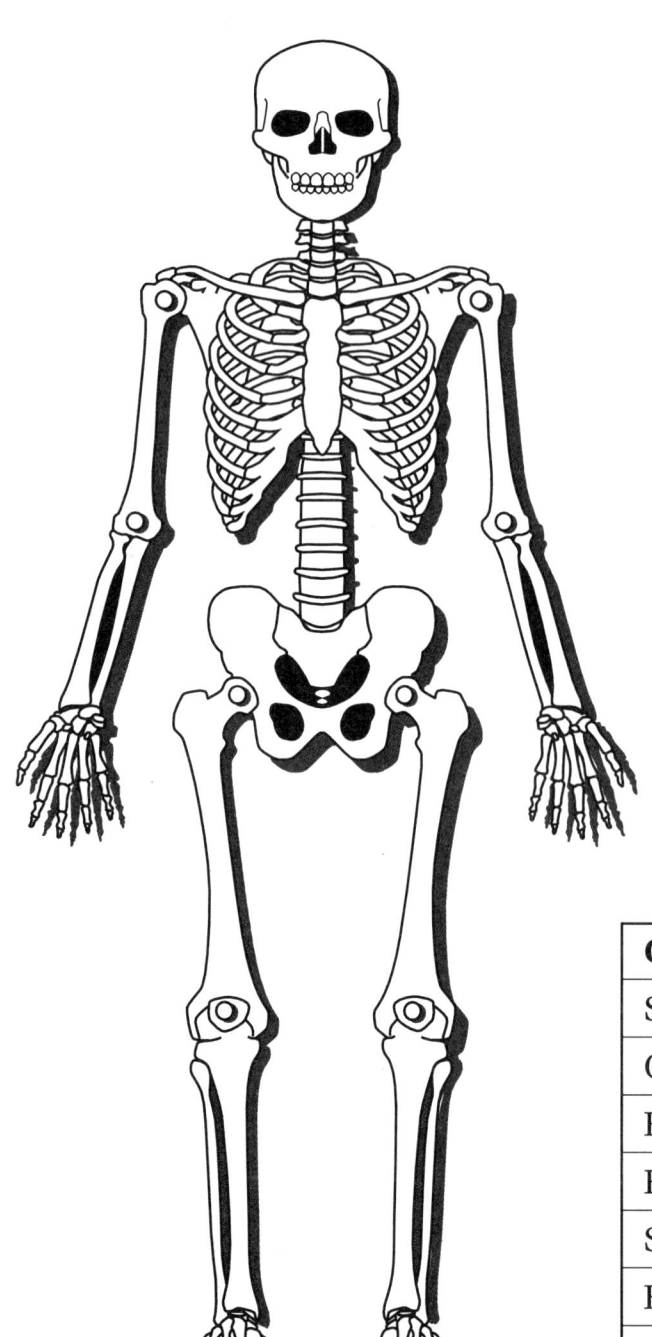

Label the bones on the diagram using this list of common bones.

Common name	Scientific name
Skull	Cranium
Collar bone	Clavicle
Breastbone	Sternum
Backbone	Vertebrae
Shoulder blade	Scapula
Hip bone	Pelvis
Thigh bone	Femur
Shin bone	Tibia
Kneecap	Patella
Forearm	made up of the Radius and Ulna
Elbow	Humerus

Science Directions Year 4 Photocopiable master © HarperCollinsPublishers Ltd 2000

Make a Model Arm Muscle

4A PM2

We have muscles in our bodies to enable us to move.

Muscles always work in pairs – as one contracts (gets shorter) the other one expands (becomes long and thin).

Follow the instructions to make a model arm muscle.

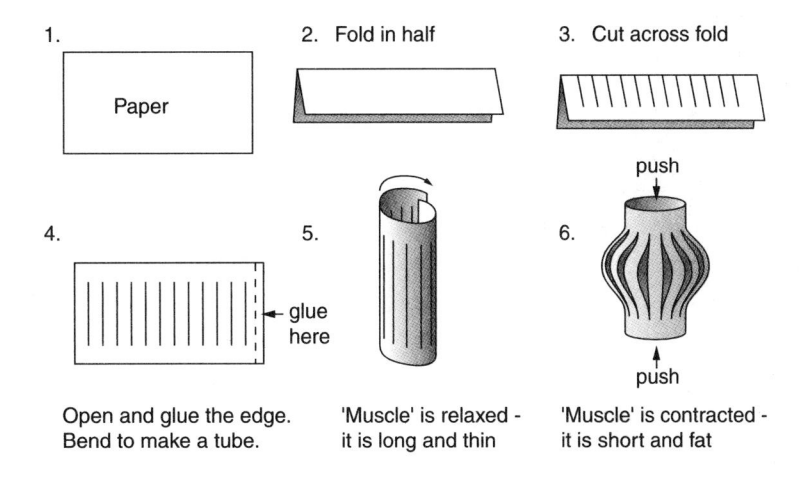

1. Paper
2. Fold in half
3. Cut across fold
4. Open and glue the edge. Bend to make a tube.
5. 'Muscle' is relaxed – it is long and thin
6. push / push — 'Muscle' is contracted – it is short and fat

Some animals have exoskeletons (bones on the outsides of their bodies).

They also have muscles inside the body to enable them to move.

Follow the instructions to make a model of an insect's leg.

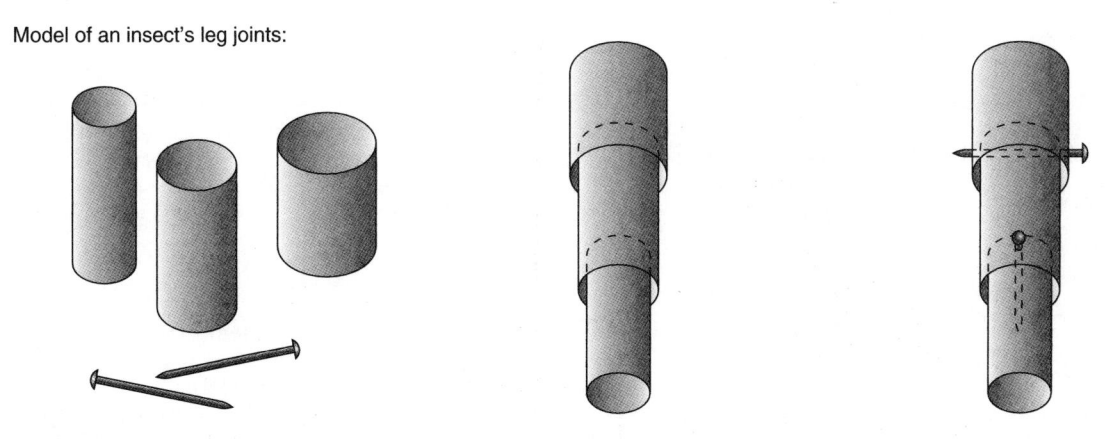

Model of an insect's leg joints:

1. You will need three cardboard tubes of differing widths, and two pins.
2. Arrange the cardboard tubes one inside the other as shown above.
3. Push the pins through the cardboard tubes at right angles to each other to create swivel joints.

Move the insect's leg around to see how it can move in a lot of different ways.

Science Directions Year 4 Photocopiable master © HarperCollins*Publishers* Ltd 2000

Long Legs

4A PM3

Name _____

My investigation to find out whether the people with the longest legs can jump the furthest or the highest

The people in my group are _____

I think that _____
(Here make a guess about what will happen.)

I am going to measure the following things.

_____

The table of my measurements will include:
name   leg length   height/length of jump

       It will look like this: Here are my results in a table.

My guess was right/wrong because _____

Here are my results on a scatter graph.

Attach your scatter graph here.

Science Directions Year 4 Photocopiable master

End of Unit Question

Adapted from KS2 Test A 1996

Muscles and Bones

Dan is thinking about what his muscles and bones do.

What must his leg muscles do to raise his foot?

Tick **one** box.

expand ☐   twist ☐

contract ☐   push ☐

Write down **two** different ways in which having a skeleton is important to humans.

1 _____

2 _____

Invertebrates

4B PM1

Science Directions Year 4 Photocopiable master © HarperCollins*Publishers* Ltd 2000

Habitat Survey

4B PM2

Sketch all the habitats you find on the walk.
The first one has been done as an example.

Name _____

Survey of _____

Name of habitat _____	Name of habitat _____
Name of habitat _____	Name of habitat _____
Name of habitat _____	Name of habitat _____

Discuss with your partner the kinds of animals and plants that live in each habitat.

Science Directions Year 4 Photocopiable master © HarperCollins*Publishers* Ltd 2000

Pond Diary

4B PM3a

How to make a pond

Written by

My pond diary

Date	Observations and maintenance

The things that have changed while I have kept my pond are

Science Directions Year 4 Photocopiable master

Pond Diary

4B
PM3b

When you have everything you need, this is what to do:

You must take care of your pond once you have made it. It is important to:

You must care for the environment you are using to set up this pond by:

The animals and plants you need to look for are:

You will need these items to make your pond:

Science Directions Year 4 Photocopiable master © HarperCollins*Publishers* Ltd 2000

End of Unit Question

Adapted from KS2 Test B 1997

4B PM4

In and Around a Pond

1. When organisms are collected from the environment they need to be treated carefully.

   Make a list of rules for the safe collection of these organisms.

   Rules for the Safe Collection of Invertebrates

   1 _____
   2 _____
   3 _____
   4 _____
   5 _____
   6 _____

2. Emma and her friends observed the animals in and around a pond.

   Which three things do all animals do?

   Tick **three** boxes.

run ☐	swim ☐	grow ☐
hunt ☐	move ☐	hear ☐
reproduce ☐	make a noise ☐	wash ☐

3. The pictures below show what some living things in a pond eat.

   | Caddis fly larva | Young tadpole | Great diving beetle larva |
   | eats young tadpoles | eats green plants | eats young tadpoles |

4. Write the names of the three living things to show one food chain in this pond.

   _____ → _____ → _____

Science Directions Year 4 Photocopiable master © HarperCollins*Publishers* Ltd 2000

Taking Temperatures

4C PM1

Predict what you think the temperatures of the substances in the table might be.

Now use a thermometer to measure the temperature of each substance. Record the results in the table.

Substance		Temperature (°C)	
		Predicted	Measured
A	Ice/water		
B	Cold tap water		
C	Hot tap water		
D	Cup of tea		
E	Cup of soup		
F	Instant noodle meal		

Draw a bar chart to show your results.

Insulators

4C PM2

Make a drawing of your experiment. Remember to label the type of material used.

Record your results in the tables

Time (minutes)	start	5	10	15	20	25
Temperature (°C)						

Total loss in temperature (°C)	

Record your results and the results of other groups in this table.

Material	Total loss in temperature (°C)

Write the materials in order, with the best insulator first and the worst insulator last.

_____ _____ _____ _____ _____
(best insulator)   (worst insulator)

Science Directions Year 4 Photocopiable master © HarperCollinsPublishers Ltd 2000

Finding the Best Insulator

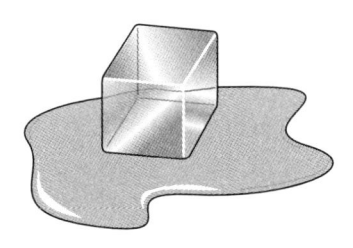

4C PM3

Planning

Which four materials are you going to test?
Which material do you think will be the best insulator? Give a reason.
How will you carry out your experiment?

Obtaining and Presenting Evidence

Present your results using a table or drawings.

Comparing Evidence and Evaluating

What have you found out?
Can you explain your results?

End of Unit Question

Adapted from KS2 Test B 1996

Temperature

John has four jars with water in them.

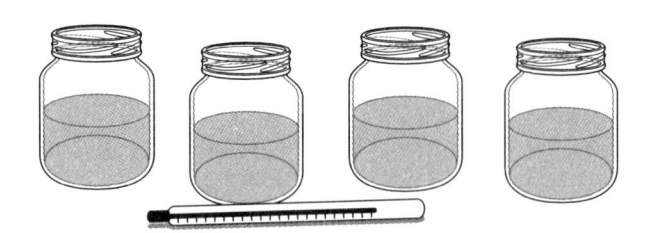

He measures the temperature of the water in each jar using a thermometer.

These are the four readings he takes.

        0°C   15°C   40°C   60°C

1 Fill in the table by putting these temperatures in the correct places.

Jar contains	Temperature of water (°C)
cool water	
water and ice	
hot water	
warm water	

2 The temperature of the classroom is always 18°C. What will happen to the ice floating in the water?

_____

3 John puts out two new jars of water. He writes the temperatures on the jars.

Next morning, the temperatures of the water in the jars have changed.

The room temperature is still 18 °C.

Write in the boxes the temperature of the water the next morning.

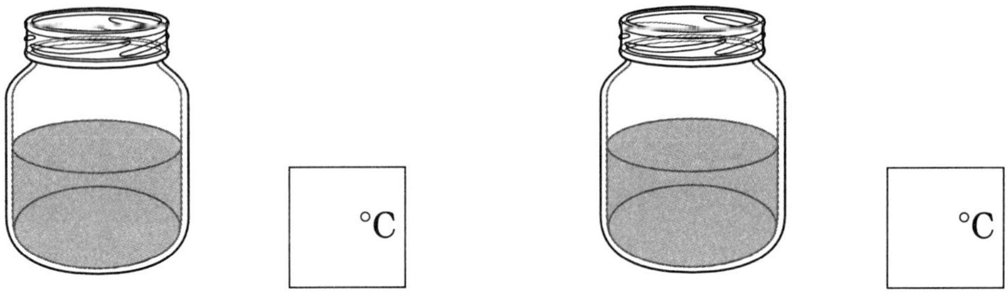

Science Directions Year 4 Photocopiable master

Solids and Liquids in the Home

4D PM1

Find some solids and liquids in your kitchen and complete the table.
Some examples have been done for you.

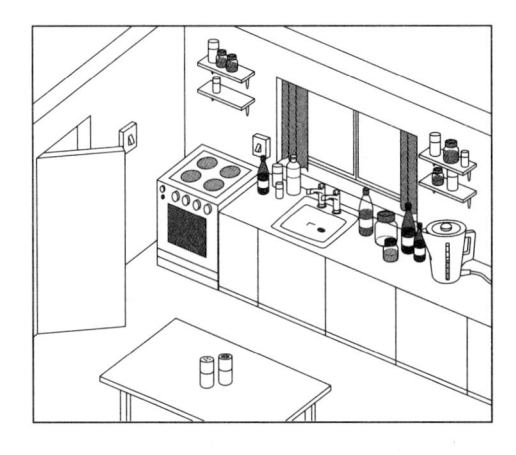

> ⚠ **Safety**
>
> Some of the substances in a kitchen can be very dangerous. You can complete the table without opening any bottles, tins or jars.
>
> If you are in doubt about what to do then ask an adult.

Type of substance	Example
Solids	
a) Solids that are powders.	1 *flour* 2 3
b) Solids made up of crystals.	1 *salt* 2 3
c) Solids made up of lumps.	1 *a bar of soap* 2 3
Liquids	
a) Liquids that are coloured.	1 *washing up liquid (yellow)* 2 3
b) Liquids that have no colour.	1 *lemonade* 2 3
c) Liquids that are not very runny.	1 *custard* 2 3

Write down **one** difference between a solid and a liquid.

_____

Science Directions Year 4 Photocopiable master © Harper*Collins*Publishers Ltd 2000

Melting Ice

4D PM2

This is an investigation to find out how quickly an ice cube melts when left in different places with different temperatures.

What you need

- three ice cubes
- three small, plastic dishes
- a thermometer
- a stopwatch

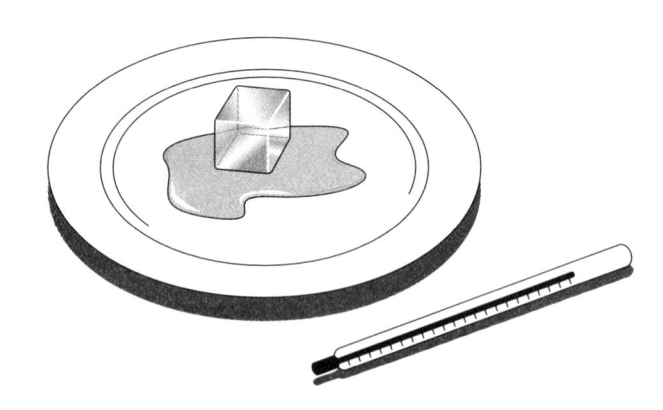

What to do

1. Choose three different places. Use the thermometer to measure the temperature of each place.
2. Collect three ice cubes and put each one on a small dish. Put one dish in each of the three places you have chosen.
3. Start your stopwatch. Every five minutes, check to see if the ice cubes have melted completely. Record your results in the table below.
4. Keep checking the ice cubes every five minutes until they have all melted.
5. Draw a line graph to show your results.

Results

Place and Temperature	Time in minutes Can you still see the ice? ✓ = yes ✗ = no												
	5	10	15	20	25	30	35	40	45	50	55	60
1 Temperature = °C												
2 Temperature = °C												
3 Temperature = °C												

Question

What do your results show?

Science Directions Year 4 Photocopiable master © HarperCollins*Publishers* Ltd 2000

Investigating Dissolving

4D PM3

This is an investigation to find out how much of a solid can be dissolved in water.

You will be testing and comparing two different solids.

Do you think the same amount of each solid will dissolve in the water?

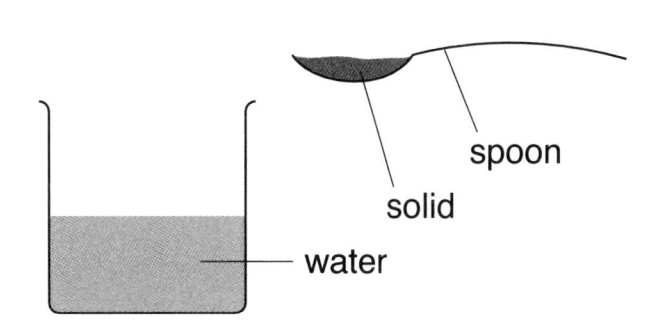

The solids you are going to compare are:

1 _____.   2 _____.

How will you measure the amount of solid that dissolves in the water?
How will you make your test fair?
Which solid do you think will dissolve the most?
Give a reason for your choice.
Draw a table to record your results.
What do your results show?

Show your results in a bar chart.

Science Directions Year 4 Photocopiable master © HarperCollins*Publishers* Ltd 2000

End of Unit Question

Adapted from KS2 Test B levels 3–5 1998

4D PM4

Liquids

Faye and Jalam are comparing liquids.

They are testing to see how quickly the liquids run down a tilted tray.

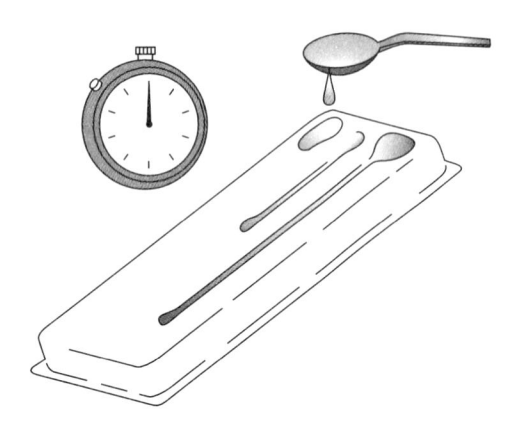

Faye put one drop of liquid on to the top of the tray.

Jalam measured how many seconds the liquid took to run 10 cm down the tray.

They did this for seven different liquids.

Here is a table of their results.

Name of liquid	Time taken (in seconds) to run 10 cm
Honey	60
Milk	
Water	5
Treacle	100
Custard	50
Cooking oil	10
Washing-up liquid	10

1. Which liquid took the longest time to run 10 cm?

2. No result has been given for milk. Predict how long you think it took.

3. How did Faye and Jalam make sure that their test was fair?

4. Jalam started to draw a bar chart of the results. Complete the bar chart.

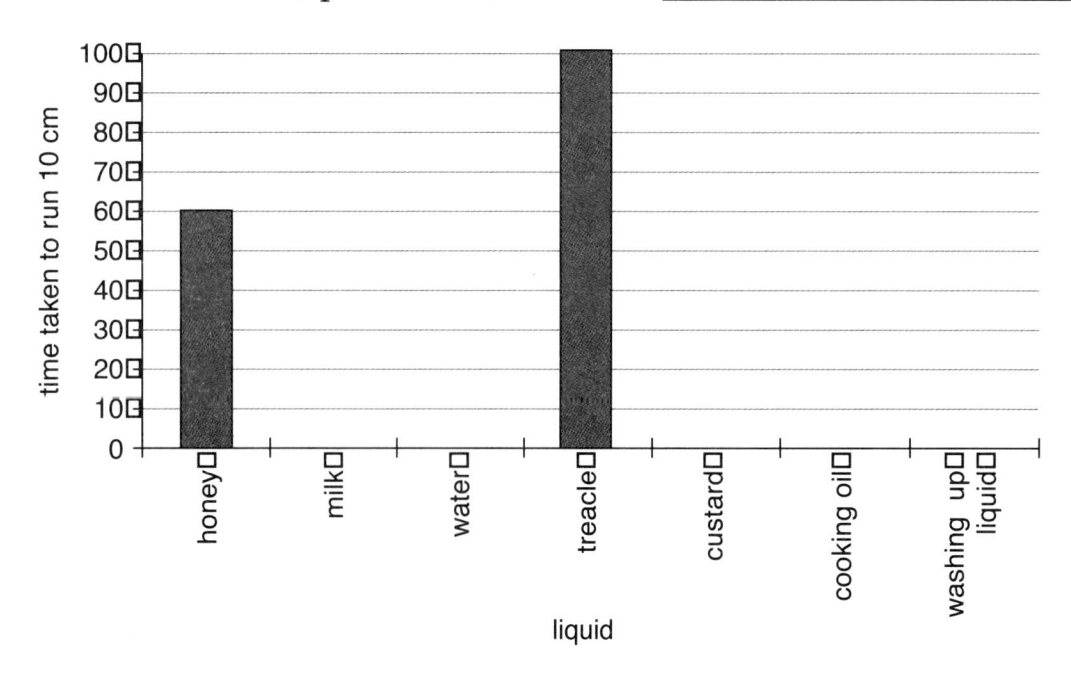

Science Directions Year 4 Photocopiable master © HarperCollins*Publishers* Ltd 2000

Friction

4E PM1

Look at the picture of the park.

Circle any part of the picture where there are friction forces.

Write a few sentences about friction.

Use the picture to help you.

_____
_____
_____
_____
_____

Science Directions Year 4 Photocopiable master © HarperCollins*Publishers* Ltd 2000

Measuring Friction Forces

4E PM2

This is an investigation to find out how much force is needed to pull different masses over different surfaces.

What you need
- a margarine tub
- masses
- a newtonmeter

What to do
1. Put one mass in the margarine tub.
2. Attach the newtonmeter to the tub.
3. Pull the tub across the surface and record the force needed to pull it.
4. Repeat for three different masses over three different surfaces.

Results

Name of surface	Mass in margarine tub (g)	Force needed to pull the tub along (N)
	1	
	2	
	3	
	1	
	2	
	3	
	1	
	2	
	3	

What do your results show?

_____

_____

Science Directions Year 4 Photocopiable master © HarperCollins*Publishers* Ltd 2000

Streamlined Shapes

4E PM3

This is an investigation to find out which is the most streamlined shape for moving through water.

What you need

- plasticene
- tall, transparent tube
- water

What to do

1 Drop a ball of plasticene into the tube of water.

2 Time how long it takes for the plasticene to sink to the bottom of the tube.

3 Change the shape of the plasticene and time it again.

4 Try five different shapes.

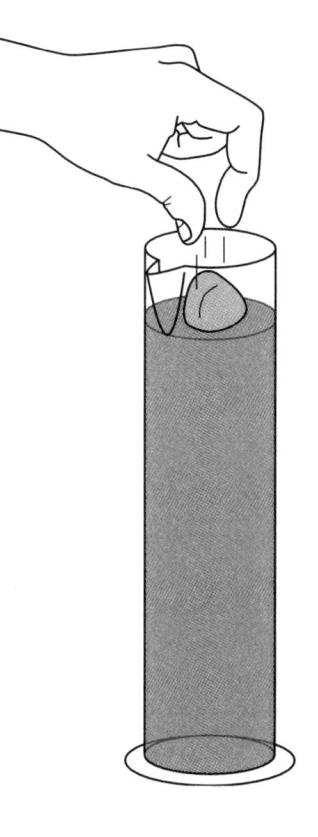

Results

Drawing of shape used	Time taken to sink to the bottom of the tube (seconds)

Which is the most streamlined shape?

Science Directions Year 4 Photocopiable master © HarperCollinsPublishers Ltd 2000

Which Shoes Give the Best Grip?

4E PM4

This is an investigation to find out which shoes give the best grip.

Planning

How will you test the shoes?
Which shoe do you predict will have the best grip? Why?
How will you make your test fair?

Results

Record your results in a table.

Shoe	Force needed to move it(N)

What have you found out?

Which shoe has the best grip?
Why do you think this shoe has the best grip?

Now draw a bar chart to show your results.

Science Directions Year 4 Photocopiable master © HarperCollins*Publishers* Ltd 2000

End of Unit Question

Adapted from KS2 Test A levels 3–5 1995

4E PM5

Forces

Lee and Sunita did an experiment to find out which footwear had the best grip.

They tied a string to a shoe. Then they put masses in the pan until the shoe just started to move.

1. Draw an arrow on the diagram to show the direction in which the shoe will move.

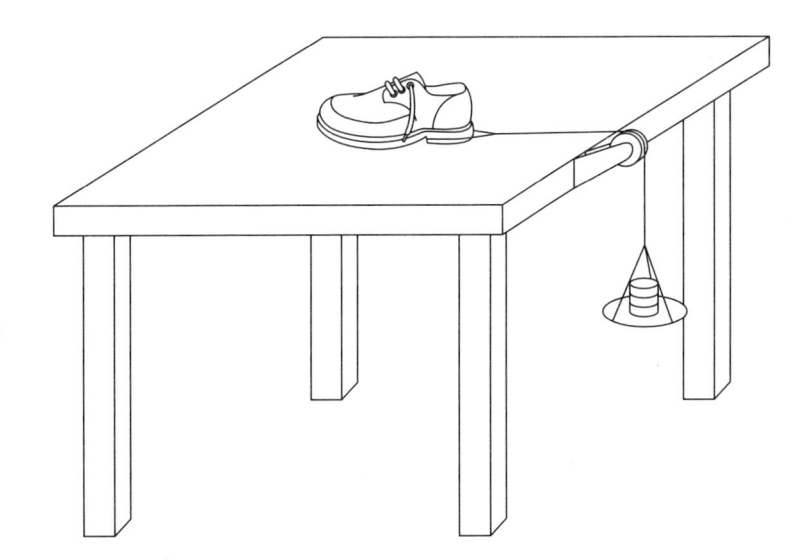

2. Name the force that is pulling downwards on the pan and the masses.

3. Name the force that stops the shoe sliding across the table.

   The children recorded their results.

Footwear	Weight in pan
shoe	440 g
trainer	310 g
rubber boot	720 g

4. How will the children use their results to decide which footwear has the best grip?

_____

_____

Science Directions Year 4 Photocopiable master © HarperCollins*Publishers* Ltd 2000

Electrical Conductors and Insulators

4F PM1

This is an investigation to test materials to see if they are electrical conductors or insulators.

What you need

- plastic covered leads
- cells and holders
- paper clips
- crocodile clips
- bulbs and holders

What to do

1 Draw the electrical circuit you are going to use.

2 Before you start testing the objects make a prediction.

3 Test the objects and complete the table.

Object	Material	Prediction ✗ or ✓		Test result ✗ or ✓	
		Conductor	Insulator	Conductor	Insulator

4 What pattern have you found in your results? _____

Making Circuits

4F PM2

Make some circuits using cells, switches, bulbs, motors and buzzers.

Draw your circuits in the spaces below.

Write about how each circuit worked.

1

2

3

4

What Affects the Brightness of a Bulb?

4F PM3

This is an investigation to find out how changing the number of cells in a circuit changes the brightness of a bulb.

Planning

Draw the circuit you are going to use.

How are you going to measure the brightness of the bulb?

How do you think the brightness of the bulb will change as you change the number of cells? Make a prediction.

Obtaining Evidence

Draw a table of your results.

Considering Evidence

What have you found out?

Use graph paper to draw a bar chart of your results.

Science Directions Year 4 Photocopiable master © HarperCollins*Publishers* Ltd 2000

End of Unit Question

Adapted from KS2 Test A levels 3–5 1998

4F PM4

Circuits

1. Lisa and James are testing different materials in a circuit.

   When they put a steel spoon in the circuit, the bulb lights.

   They put three other objects in the circuit, one at a time.

   Complete the table of results. Use one tick for each object.

   The first one has been done for you.

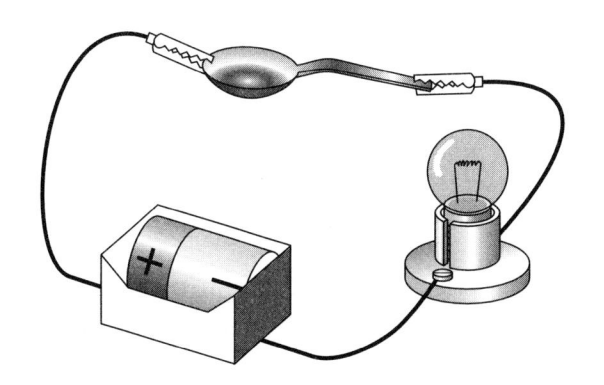

	Bulb lights	**Bulb does not light**
steel spoon	✓	
plastic comb		
wooden spoon		
aluminium foil		

2. Daniel has made a circuit.

   The circuit contains two new cells, a new bulb and a motor.

   The bulb is not lit in Daniel's circuit.

   Why is the bulb not lit in this circuit?

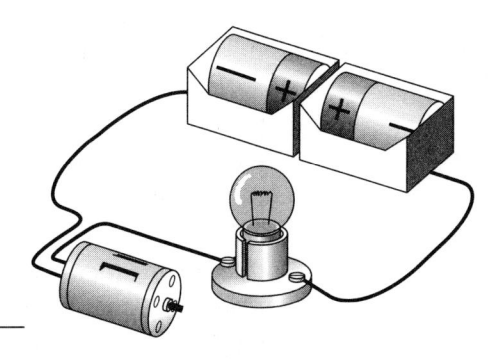

   _____

   _____

   _____

   _____

Published by HarperCollins*Publishers* Limited
77–85 Fulham Palace Road
Hammersmith
London
W6 8JB

www.CollinsEducation.com
On-line support for schools and colleges

© HarperCollins*Publishers* Limited
First published 2000 Reprinted 2001

ISBN 0 00 317 2562

Based on a scheme of work known as 'Science 3–11' developed and provided by Suffolk County Council.

Chris Sunley and Jane Bourne assert the moral right to be identified as the authors of this work.

All rights reserved. No part of this publication may be reproduced, stored in a retrieval system, or transmitted in any form or by any means, electronic, mechanical, photocopying, recording or otherwise, without either the prior permission of the Publisher or a licence permitting restricted copying in the United Kingdom issued by the Copyright Licensing Agency Ltd., 90 Tottenham Court Road, London W1P 9HE.

British Library Cataloguing in Publication Data
A catalogue record for this publication is available from the British Library

Cover: *Meredith Rainey of the US runs in the 800m heat during the World Championships at Gothenburg, Sweden, 1995.* Clive Mason/Allsport
Illustrations by Tim Oliver in association with
Cambridge Publishing Management
Design and Production by Cambridge Publishing Management

You might also like to visit
www.**fire**and**water**.com
The book lover's website

Printed by Martins The Printers, Berwick-Upon-Tweed